A Yearning toward WILD NESS

Environmental Quotations from the writings of Henry David Thoreau

Compiled and Edited
by Tim Homan

PEACHTREE PUBLISHERS, LTD.
Atlanta

Acknowledgments

I wish to extend special thanks to the following women:
Margaret Quinlin, the head workaholic at Peachtree Publishers, for supporting an
   environmentalist project and agreeing to donate a portion of its sales to The
   Nature Conservancy.
Emily Wright for her editing and superb organizational abilities.
Denise Pesti for her typing, proofing and patience.
Page Luttrell, my wife, for helping me pass judgment on quotations.

Published by
PEACHTREE PUBLISHERS, LTD.
494 Armour Circle, NE
Atlanta, Georgia 30324

Text © 1991 Tim Homan
Cover and Interior illustrations © 1991 Rusty Smith

Manufactured in the United States of America

Excerpts from Huckleberries. Holograph Lecture in his [Notes on Fruit], by Henry
David Thoreau. ©1970. Reprinted by permission of the Henry W. and Albert
A. Berg Collection. The New York Public Library. Astor, Lenox and Tilden
Foundations.

First Printing (1991)   3 9082 04777292 9

Design by Candace J. Magee
Composed by Kathryn D. Mothershed

Library of Congress Cataloging-In-Publication Data
Thoreau, Henry David, 1817-1862.
      A yearning toward wildness : environmental quotations from the
writings of Henry David Thoreau / compiled and edited by Tim Homan.
         p. cm.
      Includes index.
      ISBN 1-56145-035-9 (trade paper) : $9.95
      1. Thoreau, Henry David, 1817-1862--Quotations. 2. Nature-
-Quotations, maxims, etc. 3. Wilderness--Quotations, maxims, etc.
I. Homan, Tim. II. Title.
PS3042.H58   1991
818'.309--dc20   91-16677
                                                    CIP

Contents

Biographical Foreword / v
Introduction / vii
Editorial Comment / x
Explanation of Abbreviated Titles / x

PART 1

"In Wildness Is the Preservation of the World" / 3

"We need the tonic of wildness" / 5
"A Nature behind the ordinary" / 12
"A peculiarly wild nature" / 20
"A crusade against houses" / 34
"Take long walks" / 37
"Grow wild according to thy nature" / 41

PART 2

"Consider the Beauty of the Earth" / 49

"The point of view of wonder and awe" / 51
"The blood of the earth" / 56
"The living waters" / 60
"The circle of the seasons" / 66
"The voice of nature" / 74
"Sweet wild birds" / 78
"A wild creature" / 88
"The magical moon with attendant stars" / 99
"The beauty of the sunset or the rainbow" / 103
"Our maker, our abode, our destiny" / 108
"Matter appropriated by spirit" / 112
"The beauty of the trees" / 116

PART 3
"Let Men Tread Gently through Nature" / 127

"Sic transit gloria ruris" / 129
"Ye disgrace earth" / 136
"A finer utility" / 147
"Let us improve our opportunities" / 156

Biographical Foreword

Henry David Thoreau was born "just in the nick of time," as he phrased it, in Concord, Massachusetts, on July 12, 1817. He was born just in time to become Ralph Waldo Emerson's friend, to live during what critic Van Wyck Brooks labeled "the flowering of New England," and to enjoy the simple village life of Concord. Henry was raised in what invariably has been described as "genteel poverty." Though he was a thoughtful introvert from the beginning, his was a normal childhood of hunting, fishing, huckleberry picking, boating, running around in the woods—and reading.

In 1837 he graduated from Harvard where, despite somewhat lackadaisical study habits, he was asked to give one of the commencement addresses. In that same year Thoreau began the work of his life: his journal, a sanctum in which he carefully wrote his ideas and observations with the intention of improving his style, and to which he later returned for the material of his books and essays.

In the fall of 1839 Henry David made a two-week rowboat and walking excursion with his older brother John—an extroverted and well-liked amateur naturalist. Following his brother's death from tetanus a few years later at age twenty-five, Henry decided to write a book, a memorial, describing their trip.

On July 4, 1845, Thoreau moved to the one-room cabin he had built near the shore of the sixty-acre Walden Pond. There he wrote his first book, the narrative of his adventure with his brother: A Week on the Concord and Merrimack Rivers. And there he also recorded many of the thoughts and experiences he would later incorporate into Walden.

The poet-naturalist left Walden Pond, only a mile and a half from the center of Concord, "for as good a reason as I went there," on September 6, 1847.

After Walden, Thoreau continued his life of "plain living and high thinking" in Concord. He occasionally worked as a surveyor, a pencil maker (for his father) or an odd-job laborer. But his real work, the work we are thankful for, was learning the natural history of his native woods, fields and rivers; reading about Indians and early explorers; thinking and writing; and lecturing at the Concord Lyceum. Thoreau's thoughts and his prose, even his antislavery tracts, were closely interwoven with his walking and rowing. Soon after college graduation Henry cultivated the habit of taking long walks or rowing his boat on one of the neighborhood rivers as often as life would allow. He took his body and brain outside for inspiration; he jotted ideas and descriptions, even by moonlight, in a pocket notebook.

In addition to his almost daily walks in Concord's surrounding fields and forests, Thoreau took infrequent overnight excursions, of varying lengths, primarily to Canada, Cape Cod and New Hampshire. The greatest adventures of his life were his three canoeing and hiking expeditions to the wilderness of northern Maine.

All too soon after achieving his mature writing style, just as *Walden* began to attract enough attention for a second printing, Thoreau became ill with a bad cold, which turned into bronchitis and then developed into tuberculosis. After one last futile excursion—a doctor-recommended trip to Minnesota—Henry came back to Concord. There he died on the morning of May 6, 1862, at age forty-four. According to his friend William Ellery Channing, his last intelligible words were "moose" and "Indians."

As happens often enough to seem a prerequisite for future fame, Thoreau received little financial success or recognition from his writing while he was alive. A *Week on the Concord and Merrimack Rivers*, published at his own expense in 1849, was a commercial and artistic failure. His second and last book published while he was alive, *Walden*, was published by Ticknor and Fields at their own risk in 1854. The 2,000-book printing was not exhausted until 1859. A small reprint of *Walden* was made in 1862, after his death.

From his sickbed Henry continued to rewrite and organize manuscripts for what he knew would be posthumous publication. After his death, his sister Sophia and Channing continued the task. Three more of Thoreau's books—*The Maine Woods, Cape Cod* and *Excursions*—were published by the end of 1864.

Introduction

As a green-collar worker, a perspiring nature writer, I have read widely in natural history and related subjects over the years. The more I read, the more I encountered Henry David Thoreau as naturalist and preservationist. I discovered his ideas and quoted phrases with such frequency that I felt compelled to read the original sources: all fourteen volumes and sixty-seven hundred pages of Thoreau's journals—plus his five books and numerous essays.

Reading Thoreau was an emphatic awakening. His genius, his writing, his environmental consciousness, his love of wildness and beauty, and his personal romanticism with the earth deeply impressed me. I also came to a major realization: the cradle of American environmentalism was a rowboat rocked by the waves of Walden. This revelation came slowly and was not completed until I finished "Walking," Thoreau's "in Wildness is the preservation of the World" essay.

Until I read Thoreau, I had found no one person who qualified for the honor of being proclaimed mother or father of American environmentalism. No one else, at that early point in history, had Henry's unique combination of writing ability, twenty-first-century consciousness toward nonhuman life, daily interest in natural history, romanticism toward what he considered a living, evolving earth, plus love of wildness and beauty and ardent advocacy for the preservation of wild places, large and small.

Thoreau is also considered the founding father of the nature essay as a literary form. Henry Beston, author of *The Outermost House*, called Thoreau "the obstinate and unique genius from whom stems the great tradition of Nature writing in America." Thoreau's prose is remarkable for its capacity and desire to chisel a concept to its crystal essence—brilliant, concise, eloquent.

In his journals Thoreau wrote many remarkably descriptive passages detailing the sights of his native countryside—its lights, colors, outlines, forms, reflections and textures. Joseph Wood Krutch stated that while John Muir is our great poet of the awesome aspects of the American scene, Henry David Thoreau is our great poet of the everyday scene—the daily wonder and beauty and miracle.

Though Thoreau viewed nineteenth-century science as

spiritless and insensitive, he was, despite himself, an excellent amateur naturalist when the subjects of his study were plants— or animals that held still long enough for him to inspect them. (This statement is qualified because his avid, naked-eye bird-watching, before Roger Tory Peterson and fine optics, was unreliable by modern standards. In his defense, he steadfastly refused to shoot birds, as others did, just for the sake of identification.)

Henry learned taxonomy and botanized systematically. He recorded the yearly cycle of flower, fruit and fall. He read books on insects, investigated forest succession and conducted limnological studies of Concord's rivers and ponds. He also, primarily on his own, came to understand the ecological concept of community.

Like Bartram before him and Muir after him, the poet-naturalist Thoreau viewed nature as a continuing revelation of God. Thus his everyday walks in the Concord countryside were much more than mere naturalist ramblings: they were charged with the intense spirituality of religion. As naturalist and "self-appointed inspector of snowstorms and rainstorms," he sought both facts and phenomena—glimpses of God. And as a stoical and hard-working Puritan, Henry was a footsore seeker. He was up early and out late looking and listening, "trying to hear what was in the wind." He watched sunsets, swam in rivers at mid-night, camped on mountaintops, stayed up all night marveling at the moon and stars, listened to the strange sounds of ice expanding, walked great distances to find colonies of uncommon wildflowers. He not only took the time to smell the roses; he searched for and found the wild roses.

But Thoreau did not skip blithely across the countryside, nor was his writing confined to rural paeans. Henry was a witness, his writing a testimonial. He saw the conquest of the American wilderness from a different perspective, that of cynical chronicler and mourner. He mourned the slaughter of moose and the felling of virgin forests in his book *The Maine Woods*. He lamented Concord's loss of large animals and trees, deeply felt the resulting spiritual vacuum. He saw the beginning of an environment of humanity imploding ever further into humanity. He expressed his concern for the earth and its life—all its life, even predators and snakes.

In many respects, Thoreau was an environmental activist long before the term was invented. He decried the year-round hunting of his day, condemned loggers' dams long before the Corps of Engineers. In *A Week on the Concord and Merrimack Rivers* he publicly contemplated uncivil disobedience—putting a crowbar to a dam on behalf of the anadromous shad. Henry was censored for his "it is as immortal as I am" stand on trees more than a century before the phrase "trees have standing" became part of modern environmental parlance.

Thoreau, of course, was not the first to write of America's beauty, nor to mourn the destruction of its wilderness. But he was the first, especially in his essay "Walking," to articulate powerfully and unequivocally our physical and spiritual need for wildness—and the preservation it demands. His vision and advocacy of wildness as an essential and complementary companion to civilization became the philosophical foundation for the late nineteenth- and twentieth-century movements to preserve wild lands in America.

I collected the following environmental quotations from Thoreau's works for two principal reasons. The first is that relatively few people are familiar with Thoreau's journals or works other than *Walden* and "Civil Disobedience." As a friend jokingly remarked in response to this project: "Thoreau. Wasn't he that guy who lived in a little house next to a lake and spent a night in jail?" But even if everyone were acquainted with Henry's journals and essays, few would read them. As much as I enjoyed his journals, I will readily admit they are not for those only mildly interested in natural history and nature description. The gems do not appear one to a page. There is wading to do, time involved. Yet Thoreau remains so current and so important that I willingly compiled a drive-through Henry (one that says the world is beautiful, the world is being diminished) in hopes that his thoughts will become embossed on our convoluted brains for another century.

My most important motive in producing this book is our urgent need for Thoreau's environmental wisdom and inspiration. We are rapidly becoming unworthy of the good green earth that begot us. Environmentalism—reverence for the earth, the soil, the air, the water, the life—can no longer remain a luxury, a fad for the rich or liberal. The earth is everybody's business. A strong and steady love for our planet, plus changing how we live, buy and breed, is now an ecological necessity if we are to protect the earth for and from us. The world, as we know it today, cannot withstand another decade of environmental backsliding. Putting off solutions because they are too hard or too expensive only guarantees they will become harder and more expensive—and only guarantees that the world will increasingly become a sucked orange, a nightmare of recurring environmental disasters that no surgeon general's warning label will fit or fix. Or, as Henry said it: "We shall find our fine school house standing in a cow yard at last."

Editorial Comment

To remain true to the spirit of Thoreau's work, my publisher, my editor and I all agreed on three guiding principles. First, this book should be both a celebration and a lament. Second, Thoreau's gems should be left in their settings—as much in their original context as possible.

And last, we also felt there should be minimal editing of Thoreau's original writings. Thoreau's generation hyphenated many words that we consider one word today; we decided to remove the hyphens from only two of those words: "to-day" and "to-morrow." We also decided to change a few spellings, such as "plowing" for Thoreau's "ploughing," and to retain consistently the double "l" for words such as "travelling." Where Thoreau employed two punctuation marks together— a comma followed by a dash—we deleted the comma and retained the dash.

Explanation of Abbreviated Titles

A Week . . . . A Week on the Concord and
Merrimack Rivers

"Where I Lived" . . . . "Where I Lived, and What I Lived For"

"Former Inhabitants" . . . "Former Inhabitants; and
Winter Visitors"

"Allegash" . . . . "The Allegash and East Branch"

"Natural History" . . . . "Natural History of Massachusetts"

There is one thought for the field, another for the house. I would have my thoughts, like wild apples, to be food for walkers, and will not warrant them to be palatable if tasted in the house.

Journal
October 27, 1855

"In Wildness Is the Preservation of the World"

I WISH TO SPEAK A WORD FOR NATURE, *for absolute freedom and wildness, as contrasted with a freedom and culture merely civil—to regard man as an inhabitant or a part and parcel of Nature, rather than a member of society. I wish to make an extreme statement, if so I may make an emphatic one, for there are enough champions of civilization: the minister and the school-committee and every one of you will take care of that.*

"Walking"

"We need the tonic of wildness"

IN WILDNESS IS THE PRESERVATION OF THE WORLD. Every tree sends its fibres forth in search of the Wild. The cities import it at any price. Men plow and sail for it. From the forest and wilderness come the tonics and barks which brace mankind. Our ancestors were savages. The story of Romulus and Remus being suckled by a wolf is not a meaningless fable. The founders of every state which has risen to eminence have drawn their nourishment and vigor from a similar wild source. It was because the children of the Empire were not suckled by the wolf that they were conquered and displaced by the children of the northern forests who were.

I believe in the forest, and in the meadow, and in the night in which the corn grows.

"Walking"

WE NEED THE TONIC OF WILDNESS—to wade sometimes in marshes where the bittern and the meadow-hen lurk, and hear the booming of the snipe; to smell the whispering sedge where only some wilder and more solitary fowl builds her nest, and the mink crawls with its belly close to the ground. At the same time that we are earnest to explore and learn all things, we require that all things be mysterious and unexplorable, that land and sea be infinitely wild, unsurveyed and unfathomed by us because unfathomable. We can never have enough of Nature. We must be refreshed by the sight of inexhaustible vigor, vast and Titanic features, the sea-coast with its wrecks, the wilderness with its living and its decaying trees, the thunder cloud, and the rain which lasts three weeks and produces freshets. We need to witness our own limits transgressed, and some life pasturing freely where we never wander.

Walden, "Spring"

LIFE CONSISTS WITH WILDNESS. The most alive is the wildest. Not yet subdued to man, its presence refreshes him. One who pressed forward incessantly and never rested from his labors, who grew fast and made infinite demands on life, would always find himself in a new country or wilderness, and surrounded by the raw material of life. He would be climbing over the prostrate stems of primitive forest-trees.

Hope and the future for me are not in lawns and cultivated fields, not in towns and cities, but in the impervious and quaking swamps.

"Walking"

YES, THOUGH YOU MAY THINK ME PERVERSE, if it were proposed to me to dwell in the neighborhood of the most beautiful garden that ever human art contrived, or else of a Dismal Swamp, I should certainly decide for the swamp. How vain, then, have been all your labors, citizens, for me!

My spirits infallibly rise in proportion to the outward dreariness. Give me the ocean, the desert, or the wilderness! .... When I would recreate myself, I seek the darkest wood, the thickest and most interminable and, to the citizen, most dismal swamp. I enter a swamp as a sacred place—a *sanctum sanctorum*. There is the strength, the marrow, of Nature. The wild-wood covers the virgin-mould—and the same soil is good for men and for trees. A man's health requires as many acres of meadow to his prospect as his farm does loads of muck. There are the strong meats on which he feeds. A town is saved, not more by the righteous men in it than by the woods and swamps that surround it. A township where one primitive forest waves above while another primitive forest rots below—such a town is fitted to raise not only corn and potatoes, but poets and philosophers for the coming ages. In such a soil grew Homer and Confucius and the rest, and out of such a wilderness comes the Reformer eating locusts and wild honey.

"Walking"

THE WILDERNESS IS NEAR AS WELL AS DEAR to every man. Even the oldest villages are indebted to the border of wild wood which surrounds them, more than to the gardens of men. There is something indescribably inspiriting and beautiful in the aspect of the forest skirting and occasionally jutting into the midst of new towns, which, like the sand-heaps of fresh fox burrows, have sprung up in their midst. The very uprightness of the pines and maples asserts the ancient rectitude and vigor of nature. Our lives need the relief of such a background, where the pine flourishes and the jay still screams.

A *Week*, "Monday"

IN THIS CASE THERE WAS A CULTIVATED FIELD here some thirty years ago, but, the wood being suffered to spring up, from being open and revealed this part of the earth became a covert and concealed place. Excepting an occasional hunter who crossed it maybe once in several months, nobody has walked there, nobody has penetrated its recesses. The walker habitually goes round it, or follows the single cart-path that winds through it. Woods, both the primitive and those which are suffered to spring up in cultivated fields, thus preserve the mystery of nature. How private and sacred a place a grove thus becomes!—merely because its denseness excludes man. It is worth the while to have these thickets on various sides of the town, where the rabbit lurks and the jay builds its nest.

Journal
November 26, 1859

In literature it is only the wild that attracts us. Dullness is only another name for tameness. It is the untamed, uncivilized, free, and wild thinking in Hamlet, in the Iliad, and in all the scriptures and mythologies that delights us—not learned in the schools, not refined and polished by art. A truly good book is something as wildly natural and primitive, mysterious and marvellous, ambrosial and fertile, as a fungus or a lichen. Suppose the muskrat or beaver were to turn his views to literature, what fresh views of nature would he present! The fault of our books and other deeds is that they are too humane, I want something speaking in some measure to the condition of muskrats and skunk-cabbage as well as of men—not merely to a pining and complaining coterie of philanthropists.

Journal
November 16, 1850

Where the most beautiful wild-flowers grow, there man's spirit is fed, and poets grow.

Journal
June 15, 1852

Yet I experienced sometimes that the most sweet and tender, the most innocent and encouraging society may be found in any natural object, even for the poor misanthrope and most melancholy man. There can be no very black melancholy to him who lives in the midst of nature and has his senses still. There was never yet such a storm but it was Aeolian music to a healthy and innocent ear. Nothing can rightly compel a simple and brave man to a vulgar sadness. While I enjoy the friendship of the seasons I trust that nothing can make life a burden to me.

Walden, "Solitude"

8

THE SPRUCE, the hemlock, and the pine will not countenance despair.

"Natural History"

I AM REASSURED AND REMINDED that I am the heir of eternal inheritances which are inalienable, when I feel the warmth reflected from this sunny bank, and see the yellow sand and the reddish subsoil, and hear some dried leaves rustle and the trickling of melting snow in some sluiceway. The eternity which I detect in Nature I predicate of myself also. How many springs I have had this same experience! I am encouraged, for I recognize this steady persistency and recovery of Nature as a quality of myself.

Journal
March 23, 1856

SURELY JOY IS THE CONDITION OF LIFE. Think of the young fry that leap in ponds, the myriads of insects ushered into being on a summer evening, the incessant note of the hyla with which the woods ring in the spring, the nonchalance of the butterfly carrying accident and change painted in a thousand hues upon its wings, or the brook minnow stoutly stemming the current, the lustre of whose scales, worn bright by the attrition, is reflected upon the bank.

"Natural History"

GIVE ME THE STRONG, RANK SCENT of ferns in the spring for vigor; just blossoming late in the spring. A healthy and refined nature would always derive pleasure from the landscape. As long as the bodily vigor lasts, man sympathizes with nature.

Journal
June 27, 1852

THE INDESCRIBABLE INNOCENCE and beneficence of Nature—of sun and wind and rain, of summer and winter—such health, such cheer, they afford forever!

Walden, "Solitude"

A MILD SUMMER SUN shines over forest and lake. The earth looks as fair this morning as the Valhalla of the gods. Indeed our spirits never go beyond nature. In the woods there is an inexpressible happiness. Their mirth is but just repressed. In winter, when there is but one green leaf for many rods, what warm content is in them! They are not rude, but tender, even in the severest cold. Their nakedness is their defense. All their sounds and sights are elixir to my spirit. They possess a divine health. God is not more well. Every sound is inspiriting and fraught with the same mysterious assurance, from the creaking of the boughs in January to the soft sough of the wind in July.

Journal
December 15, 1841

TO INSURE HEALTH, a man's relation to Nature must come very near to a personal one; he must be conscious of a friendliness in her; when human friends fail or die, she must stand in the gap to him. I cannot conceive of any life which deserves the name, unless there is a certain tender relation to Nature. This it is which makes winter warm, and supplies society in the desert and wilderness. Unless Nature sympathizes with and speaks to us, as it were, the most fertile and blooming regions are barren and dreary.

Journal
January 23, 1858

MEASURE YOUR HEALTH by your sympathy with morning and spring. If there is no response in you to the awakening of nature—if the prospect of an early morning walk does not banish sleep, if the warble of the first bluebird does not thrill you—know that the morning and spring of your life are past. Thus may you feel your pulse.

Journal
February 25, 1859

SEE THE SUN RISE or set if possible each day. Let that be your pill.

Journal
November 13, 1857

WHAT IS THE PILL WHICH WILL KEEP US WELL, serene, contented? Not my or thy great-grandfather's, but our great-grandmother Nature's universal, vegetable, botanic medicines, by which she has kept herself young always, outlived so many old Parrs in her day, and fed her health with their decaying fatness. For my panacea, instead of one of those quack vials of a mixture dipped from Acheron and the Dead Sea, which come out of those long shallow black-schooner looking wagons which we sometimes see made to carry bottles, let me have a draught of undiluted morning air. Morning air! If men will not drink of this at the fountain-head of the day, why, then, we must even bottle up some and sell it in the shops, for the benefit of those who have lost their subscription ticket to morning time in this world.

Walden, "Solitude"

IN THIS FRESH EVENING each blade and leaf looks as if it had been dipped in an icy liquid greenness. Let eyes that ache come here and look—the sight will be a sovereign eyewater—or else wait and bathe them in the dark.

Journal
June 30, 1840

IT IS THE MARRIAGE OF THE SOUL WITH NATURE that makes the intellect fruitful, that gives birth to imagination. When we were dead and dry as the highway, some sense which has been healthily fed will put us in relation with Nature, in sympathy with her; some grains of fertilizing pollen, floating in the air, fall on us, and suddenly the sky is all one rainbow, is full of music and fragrance and flavor.

Journal
August 21, 1851

"A Nature
behind the
ordinary"

WE ARE SENSIBLE THAT behind the rustling leaves, and the stacks of grain, and the bare clusters of the grape, there is the field of a wholly new life, which no man has lived; that even this earth was made for more mysterious and nobler inhabitants than men and women. In the hues of October sunsets, we see the portals to other mansions than those which we occupy, not far off geographically.

A Week, "Friday"

I WAS ALWAYS CONSCIOUS OF SOUNDS IN NATURE which my ears could never hear—that I caught but the prelude to a strain. She always retreats as I advance. Away behind and behind is she and her meaning. Will not this faith and expectation make to itself ears at length? I never saw to the end, nor heard to the end; but the best part was unseen and unheard.

Journal
February 21, 1842

WE SOON GET THROUGH WITH NATURE. She excites an expectation which she cannot satisfy. The merest child which has rambled into a copsewood dreams of a wilderness so wild and strange and inexhaustible as Nature can never show him. The red-bird which I saw on my companion's string on election days I thought but the outmost sentinel of the wild, immortal camp—of the wild and dazzling infantry of the wilderness—that the deeper woods abounded with redder birds.

Journal
May 23, 1854

IT IS EASIER TO DISCOVER ANOTHER such a new world as Columbus did, than to go within one fold of this which we appear to know so well; the land is lost sight of, the compass varies, and mankind mutiny; and still history accumulates like rubbish before the portals of nature. But there is only necessary a moment's sanity and sound senses, to teach us that there is a nature behind the ordinary, in which we have only some vague preemption right and western reserve as yet. We live on the outskirts of that region. Carved wood, and floating boughs, and sunset skies are all that we know of it.

A Week, "Friday"

NATURE HAS NO HUMAN INHABITANT who appreciates her. The birds with their plumage and their notes are in harmony with the flowers, but what youth or maiden conspires with the wild luxuriant beauty of Nature? She flourishes most alone, far from the towns where they reside.

Walden, "The Ponds"

HOW LONG WE MAY HAVE GAZED on a particular scenery and think that we have seen and known it, when, at length, some bird or quadruped comes and takes possession of it before our eyes, and imparts to it a wholly new character. The heron uses these shallows as I cannot. I give them up to him.

Journal
August 14, 1859

IT WAS VAST, TITANIC, and such as man never inhabits. Some part of the beholder, even some vital part, seems to escape through the loose grating of his ribs as he ascends. He is more lone than you can imagine. There is less of substantial thought and fair understanding in him than in the plains where men inhabit. His reason is dispersed and shadowy, more thin and subtile, like the air. Vast, Titanic, inhuman Nature has got him at disadvantage, caught him alone, and pilfers him of some of his divine faculty. She does not smile on him as in the plains. She seems to say sternly, Why came ye here before your time. This ground is not prepared for you. Is it not enough that I smile in the valleys? I have never made this soil for thy feet, this air for thy breathing, these rocks for thy neighbors. I cannot pity nor fondle thee here, but forever relentlessly drive thee hence to where I *am* kind. Why seek me where I have not called thee, and then complain because you find me but a stepmother? Shouldst thou freeze or starve, or shudder thy life away, here is no shrine, nor altar, nor any access to my ear.

The Maine Woods, "Ktaadn"

[In 1846 *during the first of his three excursions to Maine, Henry climbed that state's highest peak, Mount Katahdin (5,267 ft.), one of North America's most impressive mountains. He followed game paths and stream beds—bushwhacked through and over vegetation where he had to—until he broke out onto rock above treeline. There, as he worked his way up through the boulder jumbles, Thoreau confronted the complete indifference of rock and wind and cloud-fog in the high lonesome.*]

WE HAD THUS MADE A PRETTY COMPLETE SURVEY of the top of the mountain. It is a very unique walk, and would be almost equally interesting to take though it were not elevated above the surrounding valleys. It often reminded me of my walks on the beach, and suggested how much both depend for their sublimity on solitude and dreariness. In both cases we feel the presence of some vast, titanic power. The rocks and valleys and bogs and rain-pools of the mountain are so wild and unfamiliar still that you do not recognize the one you left fifteen minutes before.

Journal
June 3, 1858

[Henry explored the crown of New Hampshire's Mount Monadnock (3,165 ft.). A monadnock is an isolated rocky hill or mountain rising above the peneplain.]

THOUGH ONCE THERE WERE MORE WHALES cast up here, I think that it was never more wild than now. We do not associate the idea of antiquity with the ocean, nor wonder how it looked a thousand years ago, as we do of the land, for it was equally wild and unfathomable always. The Indians have left no traces on its surface, but it is the same to the civilized man and the savage. The aspect of the shore only has changed. The ocean is a wilderness reaching round the globe, wilder than a Bengal jungle, and fuller of monsters, washing the very wharves of our cities and the gardens of our seaside residences. Serpents, bears, hyenas, tigers, rapidly vanish as civilization advances, but the most populous and civilized city cannot scare a shark far from its wharves.

Cape Cod,
"The Sea and the Desert"

IT IS A COUNTRY FULL OF EVERGREEN TREES, of mossy silver birches and watery maples, the ground dotted with insipid, small, red berries, and strewn with damp and moss-grown rocks—a country diversified with innumerable lakes and rapid streams, peopled with trout and various species of *leucisci*, with salmon, shad, and pickerel, and other fishes; the forest resounding at rare intervals with the note of the chickadee, the blue-jay, and the woodpecker, the scream of the fish-hawk and the eagle, the laugh of the loon, and the whistle of ducks along the solitary streams; at night, with the hooting of owls and howling of wolves; in summer, swarming with myriads of black flies and mosquitoes, more formidable than wolves to the white man. Such is the home of the moose, the bear, the caribou, the wolf, the beaver, and the Indian.

The Maine Woods, "Ktaadn"

["Leucisci" refers to a large genus of freshwater fishes including chubs, ciscos and lake herrings found mostly in the cold waters of New England and Canada. The fish hawk, as it is still often called, is the osprey.]

15

IN THE MIDDLE OF THE NIGHT, as indeed each time that we lay on the shore of a lake, we heard the voice of the loon, loud and distinct, from far over the lake. It is a very wild sound, quite in keeping with the place and the circumstances of the traveller, and very unlike the voice of a bird. I could lie awake for hours listening to it, it is so thrilling. When camping in such a wilderness as this, you are prepared to hear sounds from some of its inhabitants which will give voice to its wildness. Some idea of bears, wolves, or panthers runs in your head naturally, and when this note is first heard very far off at midnight, as you lie with your ear to the ground—the forest being perfectly still about you, you take it for granted that it is the voice of a wolf or some other wild beast, for only the last part is heard when at a distance—you conclude that it is a pack of wolves baying the moon, or, perchance, cantering after a moose. . . . It was the unfailing and characteristic sound of those lakes.

The Maine Woods, "Allegash"

I AM INTERESTED IN EACH contemporary plant in my vicinity, and have attained to a certain acquaintance with the larger ones. They are cohabitants with me of this part of the planet, and they bear familiar names. Yet how essentially wild they are! as wild, really, as those strange fossil plants whose impressions I see on my coal. Yet I can imagine that some race gathered those too with as much admiration, and knew them as intimately as I do these, that even they served for a language of the sentiments. Stigmariae stood for a human sentiment in that race's flower language. Chickweed, or a pine tree, is but little less wild. I assume to be acquainted with these, but what ages between me and the tree whose shade I enjoy! It is as if it stood substantially in a remote geological period.

Journal
June 5, 1857

THERE IT WAS, the State of Maine, which we had seen on the map, but not much like that—immeasurable forest for the sun to shine on, that eastern *stuff* we hear of in Massachusetts. No clearing, no house. It did not look as if a solitary traveller had cut so much as a walking-stick there. Countless lakes—

17

Moosehead in the southwest, forty miles long by ten wide, like a gleaming silver platter at the end of the table; Chesuncook, eighteen long by three wide, without an island; Millinocket, on the south, with its hundred islands; and a hundred others without a name; and mountains, also, whose names, for the most part, are known only to the Indians. The forest looked like a firm grass sward, and the effect of these lakes in its midst has been well compared, by one who has since visited this same spot, to that of a "mirror broken into a thousand fragments, and wildly scattered over the grass, reflecting the full blaze of the sun."

The Maine Woods, "Ktaadn"

IT IS DIFFICULT TO CONCEIVE OF A REGION UNINHABITED by man. We habitually presume his presence and influence everywhere. And yet we have not seen pure Nature, unless we have seen her thus vast and drear and inhuman, though in the midst of cities. Nature was here something savage and awful, though beautiful. I looked with awe at the ground I trod on, to see what the Powers had made there, the form and fashion and material of their work. This was that Earth of which we have heard, made out of Chaos and Old Night. Here was no man's garden, but the unhandselled globe. It was not lawn, nor pasture, nor mead, nor woodland, nor lea, nor arable, nor waste land. It was the fresh and natural surface of the planet Earth, as it was made forever and ever—to be the dwelling of man, we say—so Nature made it, and man may use it if he can. Man was not to be associated with it. It was Matter, vast, terrific—not his Mother Earth that we have heard of, not for him to tread on, or be buried in—no, it were being too familiar even to let his bones lie there—the home, this, of Necessity and Fate. There was clearly felt the presence of a force not bound to be kind to man. It was a place for heathenism and superstitious rites—to be inhabited by men nearer of kin to the rocks and to wild animals than we. We walked over it with a certain awe, stopping, from time to time, to pick the blueberries which grew there, and had a smart and spicy taste. Perchance where *our* wild pines stand, and leaves lie on their forest floor, in Concord, there were once reapers, and husbandmen planted grain;

but here not even the surface had been scarred by man, but it was a specimen of what God saw fit to make this world. What is it to be admitted to a museum, to see a myriad of particular things, compared with being shown some star's surface, some hard matter in its home! I stand in awe of my body, this matter to which I am bound has become so strange to me. I fear not spirits, ghosts, of which I am one—*that* my body might—but I fear bodies, I tremble to meet them. What is this Titan that has possession of me? Talk of mysteries! Think of our life in nature—daily to be shown matter, to come in contact with it— rocks, trees, wind on our cheeks! the *solid* earth! the *actual* world! the *common sense*! *Contact*! *Contact*! *Who* are we? *where* are we?

The Maine Woods, "Ktaadn"

"A peculiarly wild nature"

I SEEM TO SEE SOMEWHAT MORE of my own kith and kin in the lichens on the rocks than in any books. It does seem as if mine were a peculiarly wild nature, which so yearns toward all wildness. I know of no redeeming qualities in me but a sincere love for some things, and when I am reproved I have to fall back on to this ground. This is my argument in reserve for all cases. My love is invulnerable. Meet me on that ground, and you will find me strong. When I am condemned, and condemn myself utterly, I think straightway, "But I rely on my love for some things." Therein I am whole and entire. Therein I am God-propped.

Journal
December 15, 1841

AS I CAME HOME THROUGH THE WOODS with my string of fish, trailing my pole, it being now quite dark, I caught a glimpse of a woodchuck stealing across my path, and felt a strange thrill of savage delight, and was strongly tempted to seize and devour him raw; not that I was hungry then, except for that wildness which he represented. Once or twice, however, while I lived at the pond, I found myself ranging the woods, like a half-starved hound, with a strange abandonment, seeking some kind of venison which I might devour, and no morsel could have been too savage for me. The wildest scenes had become unaccountably familiar. I found in myself, and still find, an instinct toward a higher, or, as it is named, spiritual life, as do most men, and another toward a primitive rank and savage one, and I reverence them both. I love the wild not less than the good. The wildness and adventure that are in fishing still recommended it to me. I like sometimes to take rank hold on life and spend my day more as the animals do.

Walden, "Higher Laws"

I LONG FOR WILDNESS, a nature which I cannot put my foot through, woods where the wood thrush forever sings, where the hours are early morning ones, and there is dew on the grass, and the day is forever unproved, where I might have a fertile unknown for a soil about me.

Journal
June 22, 1853

I LOVE EVEN TO SEE the domestic animals reassert their native rights—any evidence that they have not wholly lost their original wild habits and vigor; as when my neighbor's cow breaks out of her pasture early in the spring and boldly swims the river, a cold, gray tide, twenty-five or thirty rods wide, swollen by the melted snow. It is the buffalo crossing the Mississippi. This exploit confers some dignity on the herd in my eyes—already dignified. The seeds of instinct are preserved under the thick hides of cattle and horses, like seeds in the bowels of the earth, an indefinite period.

"Walking"

I REJOICE THAT HORSES AND STEERS have to be broken before they can be made the slaves of men, and that men themselves have some wild oats still left to sow before they become submissive members of society. Undoubtedly, all men are not equally fit

21

subjects for civilization; and because the majority, like dogs and sheep, are tame by inherited disposition, this is no reason why the others should have their natures broken that they may be reduced to the same level.

"Walking"

WHATEVER HAS NOT come under the sway of man is wild. In this sense original and independent men are wild—not tamed and broken by society.

Journal
September 3, 1851

IT IS IN VAIN TO DREAM of a wildness distant from ourselves. There is none such. It is the bog in our brain and bowels, the primitive vigor of Nature in us, that inspires that dream. I shall never find in the wilds of Labrador any greater wildness than in some recess in Concord, i.e. than I import into it. A little more manhood or virtue will make the surface of the globe anywhere thrillingly novel and wild. That alone will provide and pay the fiddler; it will convert the district road into an untrodden cranberry bog, for it restores all things to their original primitive flourishing and promising state.

Journal
August 30, 1856

I WISH MY NEIGHBORS were wilder. A wildness whose glance no civilization could endure.

Journal
Early March, 1851

I SHOULD BE PLEASED to meet man in the woods. I wish he were to be encountered like wild caribous and moose.

Journal
June 18, 1840

AH, BLESS THE LORD, O my soul! bless him for wildness, for crows that will not alight within gunshot!

Journal
January 12, 1855

22

I LOVE TO SEE THAT NATURE is so rife with life that myriads can be afforded to be sacrificed and suffered to prey on one another; that tender organizations can be so serenely squashed out of existence like pulp—tadpoles which herons gobble up, and tortoises and toads run over in the road; and that sometimes it has rained flesh and blood! With the liability to accident, we must see how little account is to be made of it.

Walden, "Spring"

THE ENERGY AND EXCITEMENT of the musquash-hunter even, not despairing of life, but keeping the same rank and savage hold on it that his predecessors have for so many generations, while so many are sick and despairing, even this is inspiriting to me.

Journal
January 22, 1859

I WENT TO THE WOODS BECAUSE I wished to live deliberately, to front only the essential facts of life, and see if I could learn what it had to teach, and not, when I came to die, discover that I had not lived. I did not wish to live what was not life, living is so dear; nor did I wish to practice resignation, unless it was quite necessary. I wanted to live deep and suck out all the marrow of life, to live so sturdily and Spartan-like as to put to rout all that was not life, to cut a broad swath and shave close, to drive life into a corner, and reduce it to its lowest terms, and, if it proved to be mean, why then to get the whole and genuine meanness of it, and publish its meanness to the world; or if it were sublime, to know it by experience, and be able to give a true account of it in my next excursion.

Walden, "Where I Lived"

MY DESIRE FOR KNOWLEDGE is intermittent; but my desire to commune with the spirit of the universe, to be intoxicated even with the fumes, call it, of that divine nectar, to bear my head through atmospheres and over heights unknown to my feet, is perennial and constant.

Journal
February 9, 1851

I DISCOVERED MANY A SITE FOR A HOUSE not likely to be soon improved, which some might have thought too far from the village, but to my eyes the village was too far from it. Well, there I might live, I said; and there I did live, for an hour, a summer and a winter life; saw how I could let the years run off, buffet the winter through, and see the spring come in. The future inhabitants of this region, wherever they may place their houses, may be sure that they have been anticipated. An afternoon sufficed to lay out the land into orchard, wood lot, and pasture, and to decide what fine oaks or pines should be left to stand before the door, and whence each blasted tree could be seen to the best advantage; and then I let it lie, fallow perchance, for a man is rich in proportion to the number of things which he can afford to let alone.

Walden, "Where I Lived"

I SOON FOUND MYSELF OBSERVING when plants first blossomed and leafed, and I followed it up early and late, far and near, several years in succession, running to different sides of the town and into the neighboring towns, often between twenty and thirty miles in a day. I often visited a particular plant four or five miles distant, half a dozen times within a fortnight, that I might know exactly when it opened, beside attending to a great many others in different directions and some of them equally distant, at the same time. At the same time I had an eye for birds and whatever else might offer.

Journal
December, 1856

TO ANTICIPATE, not the sunrise and the dawn merely, but, if possible, Nature herself! How many mornings, summer and winter, before yet any neighbor was stirring about his business, have I been about mine! No doubt, many of my townsmen have met me returning from this enterprise, farmers starting for Boston in the twilight, or woodchoppers going to their work. It is true, I never assisted the sun materially in his rising, but, doubt not, it was of the last importance only to be present at it.

So many autumn, ay, and winter days, spent outside the town, trying to hear what was in the wind, to hear and carry it express! I well-nigh sunk all my capital in it, and lost my own breath into the bargain, running in the face of it. If it had concerned either of the political parties, depend upon it, it would have appeared in the Gazette with the earliest intelligence. At other times watching from the observatory of some cliff or tree, to telegraph any new arrival; or waiting at evening on the hilltops for the sky to fall, that I might catch something, though I never caught much, and that, manna-wise, would dissolve again in the sun. . . .

For many years I was self-appointed inspector of snow storms and rain storms, and did my duty faithfully; surveyor, if not of highways, then of forest paths and all across-lot routes, keeping them open, and ravines bridged and passable at all seasons, where the public heel had testified to their utility.

Walden, "Economy"

MY PROFESSION is to be always on the alert to find God in nature, to know his lurking-places, to attend all the oratorios, the operas, in nature.

Journal
September 7, 1851

IT IS CERTAINLY IMPORTANT that there be some priests, some worshippers of Nature.

Journal
April 9, 1856

THE POET IS NO TENDER SLIP of fairy stock, who requires peculiar institutions and edicts for his defence, but the toughest son of earth and of Heaven, and by his greater strength and endurance his fainting companions will recognize the God in him. It is the worshippers of beauty, after all, who have done the real pioneer work of the world.

A Week, "Friday"

BUT THERE ARE SPIRITS of a yet more liberal culture, to whom no simplicity is barren. There are not only stately pines, but fragile flowers, like the orchises, commonly described as too delicate for cultivation, which derive their nutriment from the crudest mass of peat. These remind us, that, not only for strength, but for beauty, the poet must, from time to time, travel the logger's path and the Indian's trail, to drink at some new and more bracing fountain of the Muses, far in the recesses of the wilderness.

The Maine Woods,
"Chesuncook"

IT IS WORTH THE WHILE to have lived a primitive wilderness life at some time, to know what are, after all, the necessaries of life and what methods society has taken to supply them.

Journal
1845-1846

WHEN IT WAS PROPOSED TO ME to go abroad, rub off some rust, and *better my condition* in a worldly sense, I fear lest my life will lose some of its homeliness. If these fields and streams and woods, the phenomena of nature here, and the simple occupations of the inhabitants should cease to interest and inspire me, no culture or wealth would atone for the loss. I fear the dissipation that travelling, going into society, even the best, the enjoyment of intellectual luxuries, imply. If Paris is much in your mind, if it is more and more to you, Concord is less and less, and yet it would be a wretched bargain to accept the proudest Paris in exchange for my native village. At best, Paris could only be a school in which to learn to live here, a stepping-stone to Concord, a school in which to fit for this university. I wish so to live ever as to derive my satisfactions and inspirations from the commonest events, every-day phenomena, so that what my senses hourly perceive, my daily walk, the conversation of my neighbors, may inspire me, and I may dream of no heaven but that which lies about me. A man may acquire a taste for wine or brandy, and so lose his love for water, but should we not pity him?

The sight of a marsh hawk in Concord meadows is worth more to me than the entry of the allies into Paris. In this sense I am not ambitious. I do not wish my native soil to become exhausted and run out through neglect. Only that travelling is good which reveals to me the value of home and enables me to enjoy it better. That man is the richest whose pleasures are the cheapest.

Journal
March 11, 1856

I HAVE GIVEN MYSELF UP TO NATURE; I have lived so many springs and summers and autumns and winters as if I had nothing else to do but *live* them, and imbibe whatever nutriment they had for me; I have spent a couple of years, for instance, with the flowers chiefly, having none other so binding engagement as to observe when they opened; I could have afforded to spend a whole fall observing the changing tints of the foliage. Ah, how I have thriven on solitude and poverty! I cannot overstate this advantage. I do not see how I could have enjoyed it, if the public had been expecting as much of me as there is danger now that they will. If I go abroad lecturing, how shall I ever recover the lost winter?

Journal
September 19, 1854

HERE IS THIS VAST, SAVAGE, HOWLING mother of ours, Nature, lying all around, with such beauty, and such affection for her children, as the leopard; and yet we are so early weaned from her breast to society, to that culture which is exclusively an interaction of man on man—a sort of breeding in and in, which produces at most a merely English nobility, a civilization destined to have a speedy limit.

"Walking"

I DO NOT VALUE any view of the universe into which man and the institutions of man enter very largely and absorb much of the attention. Man is but the place where I stand, and the prospect hence is infinite. It is not a chamber of mirrors which reflect me.

Journal
April 2, 1852

28

MANKIND IS A GIGANTIC institution; it is a community to which most men belong. It is a test I would apply to my companion— can he forget man? can he see this world slumbering?

Journal
April 2, 1852

AFTER HAVING SOME BUSINESS DEALINGS with men, I am occasionally chagrined, and feel as if I had done some wrong, and it is hard to forget the ugly circumstance. I see that such intercourse long continued would make one thoroughly prosaic, hard, and coarse. But the longest intercourse with Nature, though in her rudest moods, does not thus harden and make coarse. A hard, insensible man whom we liken to a rock is indeed much harder than a rock. From hard, coarse, insensible men with whom I have no sympathy, I go to commune with the rocks, whose hearts are comparatively soft.

Journal
November 15, 1853

THE WORLD WILL NEVER FIND OUT why you don't love to have your bed tucked up for you—why you will be so perverse. I enjoy more drinking water at a clear spring than out of a goblet at a gentleman's table. I like best the bread which I have baked, the garment which I have made, the shelter which I have constructed, the fuel which I have gathered.

Journal
October 20, 1855

I HAVE FOUND MYSELF AS WELL OFF when I have fallen into a quagmire, as in an armchair in the most hospitable house. The prospect was pretty much the same. Without anxiety let us wander on, admiring whatever beauty the woods exhibit.

Journal
1850

IN SOCIETY YOU WILL NOT FIND HEALTH, but in nature. You must converse much with the field and woods, if you would imbibe such health into your mind and spirit as you covet for your body. Society is always diseased, and the best is the sickest. There is no scent in it so wholesome as that of the pines, nor any fragrance so penetrating and restorative as that of ever-lasting in high pastures. Without that our feet at least stood in the midst of nature, all our faces would be pale and livid.

I should like to keep some book of natural history always by me as a sort of elixir, the reading of which would restore the tone of my system and secure me true and cheerful views of life. For to the sick, nature is sick, but to the well, a fountain of health. To the soul that contemplates some trait of natural beauty no harm nor disappointment can come. The doctrines of despair, of spiritual or political servitude, no priestcraft nor tyranny, was ever taught by such as drank in the harmony of nature.

Journal
December 31, 1841

WOULD IT NOT BE A LUXURY to stand up to one's chin in some retired swamp for a whole summer's day, scenting the sweet-fern and bilberry blows, and lulled by the minstrelsy of gnats and mosquitoes? A day passed in the society of those Greek sages, such as described in the "Banquet" of Xenophon, would not be comparable with the dry wit of decayed cranberry vines, and the fresh Attic salt of the moss beds. Say twelve hours of genial and familiar converse with the leopard frog. The sun to rise behind alder and dogwood, and climb buoyantly to his meridian of three hands' breadth, and finally sink to rest behind some bold western hummock. To hear the evening chant of the mosquito from a thousand green chapels, and the bittern begin to boom from his concealed fort like a sunset gun!

Journal
June 16, 1840

AND YET THERE IS NO more tempting novelty than this new No-vember. No going to Europe or another world is to be named with it. Give me the old familiar walk, post-office and all, with this ever new self, with this infinite expectation and faith, which does not know when it is beaten. We'll go nutting once more. We'll pluck the nut of the world, and crack it in the winter evenings. Theatres and all other sightseeing are puppet-shows in comparison. I will take another walk to the Cliff, another row on the river, another skate on the meadow, be out in the first snow, and associate with the winter birds. Here I am at home. In the bare and bleached crust of the earth I recognize my friend.

Journal
November 1, 1858

IF THE DAY AND THE NIGHT are such that you greet them with joy, and life emits a fragrance like flowers and sweet-scented herbs, is more elastic, more starry, more immortal—that is your success. All nature is your congratulation, and you have cause momentarily to bless yourself. The greatest gains and values are farthest from being appreciated. We easily come to doubt if they exist. We soon forget them. They are the highest reality. Perhaps the facts most astounding and most real are never communicated by man to man. The true harvest of my daily life is somewhat as intangible and indescribable as the tints of morning or evening. It is a little star-dust caught, a segment of the rainbow which I have clutched.

Walden, "Higher Laws"

IN ORDER TO AVOID delusions, I would fain let man go by and behold a universe in which man is but as a grain of sand.

Journal
April 2, 1852

HOW IMPORTANT IS a constant intercourse with nature and the contemplation of natural phenomena to the preservation of moral and intellectual health! The discipline of the schools or of business can never impart such serenity to the mind.

Journal
May 6, 1851

THERE IS NOTHING SO SANATIVE, SO POETIC, as a walk in the woods and fields even now, when I meet none abroad for pleasure. Nothing so inspires me and excites such serene and profitable thought. The objects are elevating. In the street and in society I am almost invariably cheap and dissipated, my life is unspeakably mean. No amount of gold or respectability would in the least redeem it—dining with the Governor or a member of Congress!! But alone in distant woods or fields, in unpretending sprout-lands or pastures tracked by rabbits, even in a bleak and, to most, cheerless day, like this, when a villager would be thinking of his inn, I come to myself, I once more feel myself grandly related, and that cold and solitude are friends of mine. I suppose that this value, in my case, is equivalent to what others get by churchgoing and prayer. I come to my solitary woodland walk as the homesick go home. I thus dispose of the superfluous and see things as they are, grand and beauti-ful. . . . I get away a mile or two from the town into the stillness and solitude of nature, with rocks, trees, weeds, snow about me. I enter some glade in the woods, perchance, where a few weeds and dry leaves alone lift themselves above the surface of the snow, and it is as if I had come to an open window. I see out and around myself. . . . This stillness, solitude, wildness of nature is a kind of thoroughwort, or boneset, to my intellect. This is what I go out to seek. It is as if I always met in those places some grand, serene, immortal, infinitely encouraging, though invisible, companion, and walked with him. There at last my nerves are steadied, my senses and my mind do their office. I am aware that most of my neighbors would think it a hardship to be compelled to linger here one hour, especially this bleak day, and yet I receive this sweet and ineffable compensation for it. It is the most agreeable thing I do. Truly, my coins are uncurrent with them.

I love and celebrate nature, even in detail, merely because I love the scenery of these interviews and translations. I love to remember every creature that was at this *club*. I thus get off a certain social scurf and scaliness. I do not consider the other animals brutes in the common sense. I am attracted toward them undoubtedly because I never heard any nonsense from them. I have not convicted them of folly, or vanity, or pompos-ity, or stupidity, in dealing with me. Their vices, at any rate, do not interfere with me. My fairies invariably take to flight when a man appears upon the scene. In a caucus, a meeting-house, a lyceum, a clubroom, there is nothing like it in my experience. But away out of the town, on Brown's scrub oak lot, which was sold the other day for six dollars an acre, I have company such as England cannot buy, nor afford. This society is what I live, what I survey, for. I subscribe generously to *this*—all that I have and am.

Journal
January 7, 1857

"A crusade against houses"

MEN NOWHERE, EAST OR WEST, live yet a *natural* life, round which the vine clings, and which the elm willingly shadows. Man would desecrate it by his touch, and so the beauty of the world remains veiled to him. He needs not only to be spiritualized, but *naturalized*, on the soil of earth. Who shall conceive what kind of roof the heavens might extend over him, what seasons minister to him, and what employment dignify his life!

A Week, "Friday"

IT IS VERY RARE that I hear one express a strong and imperishable attachment to a particular scenery, or to the whole of nature—I mean such as will control their whole lives and characters. . . . Most are tender and callow creatures that wear a house as their outmost shell and must get their lives insured when they step abroad from it. They are lathed and plastered in from all natural influences, and their delicate lives are a long battle with the dyspepsia. . . . How rarely a man's love for nature becomes a ruling principle with him, like a youth's affection for a maiden, but more enduring! All nature is my bride.

Journal
April 23, 1857

WINTER HAS COME unnoticed by me, I have been so busy writing. This is the life most lead in respect to Nature. How different from my habitual one! It is hasty, coarse, and trivial, as if you were a spindle in a factory. The other is leisurely, fine, and glorious, like a flower. In the first case you are merely getting your living; in the second you live as you go along. You travel only on roads of the proper grade without jar or running off the track, and sweep round the hills by beautiful curves.

Journal
December 8, 1854

VERY FEW MEN CAN speak of Nature with any truth. They confer no favor; they do not speak a good word for her. Most cry better than they speak. You can get more nature out of them by pinching than by addressing them. It is naturalness, and not simply good nature, that interests. I like better the surliness with which the woodchopper speaks of his woods, handling them as indifferently as his axe, than the mealy-mouthed enthusiasm of the lover of nature.

Journal
March 13, 1841

THE CIVILIZED MAN HAS the habits of the house. His house is a prison, in which he finds himself oppressed and confined, not sheltered and protected. He walks as if he sustained the roof; he carries his arms as if the walls would fall in and crush him, and his feet remember the cellar beneath. His muscles are never relaxed. It is rare that he overcomes the house, and learns to sit at home in it, and roof and floor and walls support themselves, as the sky and trees and earth.

Journal
April 26, 1841

A GREAT PART of our troubles are literally domestic or originate in the house and from living indoors. I could write an essay to be entitled "Out of Doors"—undertake a crusade against houses. What a different thing Christianity preached to the house-bred and to a party who lived out of doors!

Journal
April 26, 1857

THE UNIVERSE IS LARGER THAN ENOUGH for man's abode. Some rarely go outdoors, most are always at home at night, very few indeed have stayed out all night once in their lives, fewer still have gone behind the world of humanity, seen its institutions like toadstools by the wayside.

Journal
April 2, 1852

WHAT SHALL WE DO with a man who is afraid of the woods, their solitude and darkness? What salvation is there for him?

Journal
November 16, 1850

THERE ARE VARIOUS DEGREES of living out-of-doors. You must be outdoors long, early and late, and travel far and earnestly, in order to perceive the phenomena of the day. Even then much will escape you. Few live so far outdoors as to hear the first geese go over.

Journal
September 13, 1859

WE MUST GO OUT and re-ally ourselves to Nature every day. We must make root, send out some little fibre at least, even every winter day. I am sensible that I am imbibing health when I open my mouth to the wind. Staying in the house breeds a sort of insanity always. Every house is in this sense a hospital. A night and a forenoon is as much confinement to those wards as I can stand. I am aware that I recover some sanity which I had lost almost the instant that I come abroad.

Journal
December 29, 1856

"Take long walks"

IT IS IMPORTANT, THEN, that we should air our lives from time to time by removals, and excursions into the fields and woods—starve our vices. Do not sit so long over any cellar-hole as to tempt your neighbor to bid for the privilege of digging salt-petre there.

Journal
September 23, 1859

TAKE LONG WALKS in stormy weather or through deep snows in the fields and woods, if you would keep your spirits up. Deal with brute nature. Be cold and hungry and weary.

Journal
December 25, 1856

BUT NO WEATHER INTERFERED fatally with my walks, or rather my going abroad, for I frequently tramped eight or ten miles through the deepest snow to keep an appointment with a beech-tree, or a yellow-birch, or an old acquaintance among the pines.

Walden, "Former Inhabitants"

IT IS A CERTAIN FAERYLAND where we live. You may walk out in any direction over the earth's surface, lifting your horizon, and everywhere your path, climbing the convexity of the globe, leads you between heaven and earth, not away from the light of the sun and stars and the habitations of men. I wonder that I ever get five miles on my way, the walk is so crowded with events and phenomena.

Journal
June 7, 1851

I THINK THAT I CANNOT PRESERVE my health and spirits, unless I spend four hours a day at least—and it is commonly more than that—sauntering through the woods and over the hills and fields, absolutely free from all worldly engagements.

"Walking"

AND THEN FOR MY AFTERNOON WALKS I have a garden, larger than any artificial garden that I have read of and far more attractive to me—mile after mile of embowered walks, such as no noble-man's grounds can boast, with animals running free and wild therein as from the first—varied with land and water prospect, and, above all, so retired that it is extremely rare that I meet a single wanderer in its mazes. No gardener is seen therein, no gates nor fences. You may wander away to solitary bowers and brooks and hills.

Journal
June 20, 1850

WHEN WE WALK, we naturally go to the fields and woods: what would become of us, if we walked only in a garden or a mall?

"Walking"

I AM ALARMED WHEN it happens that I have walked a mile into the woods bodily, without getting there in spirit. In my afternoon walk I would fain forget all my morning occupations and my obligations to society. But it sometimes happens that I cannot easily shake off the village. The thought of some work will run in my head and I am not where my body is—I am out of my senses. In my walks I would fain return to my senses. What business have I in the woods, if I am thinking of something out of the woods?

"Walking"

WHEN YOU THINK THAT your walk is profitless and a failure, and you can hardly persuade yourself not to return, it is on the point of being a success, for then you are in that subdued and knocking mood to which Nature never fails to open.

Journal
January 27, 1860

I KNOW OF BUT ONE OR TWO PERSONS with whom I can afford to walk. With most the walk degenerates into a mere vigorous use of your legs, ludicrously purposeless, while you are discussing some mighty argument, each one having his say, spoiling each other's day, worrying one another with conversation, hustling one another with our conversation. I know of no use in the walking part in this case, except that we may seem to be getting on together toward some goal; but of course we keep our original distance all the way. Jumping every wall and ditch with vigor in the vain hope of shaking your companion off. Trying to kill two birds with one stone, though they sit at opposite points of the compass, to see nature and do the honors to one who does not.

Journal
November 8, 1858

BUT THE WALKING OF WHICH I SPEAK has nothing in it akin to taking exercise, as it is called, as the sick take medicine at stated hours—as the swinging of dumb-bells or chairs; but is itself the enterprise and adventure of the day. If you would get exercise, go in search of the springs of life. Think of a man's swinging dumb-bells for his health, when those springs are bubbling up in far-off pastures unsought by him!

"Walking"

WE SHOULD GO FORTH on the shortest walk, perchance, in the spirit of undying adventure, never to return—prepared to send back our embalmed hearts only as relics to our desolate kingdoms. If you are ready to leave father and mother, and brother and sister, and wife and child and friends, and never see them again—if you have paid your debts, and made your will, and settled all your affairs, and are a free man, then you are ready for a walk.

"Walking"

NO WEALTH CAN BUY the requisite leisure, freedom, and independence which are the capital in this profession. It comes only by the grace of God. It requires a direct dispensation from Heaven to become a walker. You must be born into the family of the Walkers.

"Walking"

"Grow wild according to thy nature"

REMEMBER THY CREATOR in the days of thy youth. Rise free from care before the dawn, and seek adventures. Let the noon find thee by other lakes, and the night overtake thee everywhere at home. There are no larger fields than these, no worthier games than may here be played. Grow wild according to thy nature, like these sedges and brakes, which will never become English hay. Let the thunder rumble; what if it threaten ruin to farmers' crops? that is not its errand to thee. Take shelter under the cloud, while they flee to carts and sheds. Let not to get a living by thy trade, but thy sport. Enjoy the land. . . .

Walden, "Baker Farm"

EACH MAN'S NECESSARY PATH, though as obscure and apparently uneventful as that of a beetle in the grass, is the way to the deepest joys he is susceptible of; though he converses only with moles and fungi and disgraces his relatives, it is no matter if he knows what is steel to his flint.

Journal
November 18, 1857

Pursue some path, however narrow and crooked, in which you can walk with love and reverence. Wherever a man separates from the multitude and goes his own way, there is a fork in the road, though the travellers along the highway see only a gap in the paling.

Journal
October 18, 1855

Keep strictly onward in that path alone which your genius points out. Do the things which lie nearest to you, but which are difficult to do. Live a purer, a more thoughtful and laborious life, more true to your friends and neighbors, more noble and magnanimous, and that will be better than a wild walk.

Journal
January 12, 1852

Be rather the Mungo Park, the Lewis and Clark and Frobisher, of your own streams and oceans; explore your own higher latitudes—with shiploads of preserved meats to support you, if they be necessary; and pile the empty cans sky-high for a sign. Were preserved meats invented to preserve meat merely? Nay, be a Columbus to whole new continents and worlds within you, opening new channels, not of trade, but of thought. Every man is the lord of a realm beside which the earthly empire of the Czar is but a petty state, a hummock left by the ice.

Walden, Conclusion

Be resolutely and faithfully what you are; be humbly what you aspire to be. Be sure you give men the best of your wares, though they be poor enough, and the gods will help you to lay up a better store for the future. Man's noblest gift to man is his sincerity, for it embraces his integrity also. Let him not dole out of himself anxiously, to suit their weaker or stronger stomachs, but make a clean gift of himself, and empty his coffers at once.

Journal
January 24, 1841

To LIVE IN RELATIONS of truth and sincerity with men is to dwell in a frontier country. What a wild and unfrequented wilderness that would be!

Journal
January 12, 1852

LIVE IN EACH SEASON as it passes; breathe the air, drink the drink, taste the fruit, and resign yourself to the influences of each. Let these be your only diet-drink and botanical medicines. . . .

Be blown on by all the winds. Open all your pores and breathe in all the tides of nature, in all her streams and oceans, at all seasons. . . .

Grow green with spring—yellow and ripe with autumn. Drink of each season's influence as a vial, a true panacea of all remedies mixed for your especial use. The vials of summer never made a man sick, only those which he had stored in his cellar. Drink the wines not of your own but of nature's bottling—not kept in a goat- or pig-skin, but in the skins of a myriad fair berries.

Let Nature do your bottling, as also your pickling and preserving.

For all nature is doing her best each moment to make us well. She exists for no other end. Do not resist her. With the least inclination to be well we should not be sick. Men have discovered, or think that they have discovered the salutariness of a few wild things only, and not of all nature. Why nature is but another name for health.

"Huckleberries"

IT WOULD BE WORTH THE WHILE to ask ourselves weekly, Is our life innocent enough? Do we live *inhumanely*, toward man or beast, in thought or act? To be serene and successful we must be at one with the universe. The least conscious and needless injury inflicted on any creature is to its extent a suicide. What peace—or life—can a murderer have?

Journal
May 28, 1854

IT IS NOT BY A COMPROMISE, it is not by a timid and feeble repentance, that a man will save his soul and *live*, at last. He has got to *conquer* a clear field, letting Repentance & Co. go. That's a well-meaning but weak firm that has assumed the debts of an old and worthless one. You are to fight in a field where no allowances will be made, no courteous bowing to one-handed knights. You are expected to do your duty, not in spite of every thing but *one*, but in spite of *everything*.

Journal
September 24, 1859

WHY NOT LIVE A HARD and emphatic life, not to be avoided, full of adventures and work, learn much in it, travel much, though it be only in these woods? I sometimes walk across a field with unexpected expansion and long-missed content, as if there were a field worthy of me. The usual daily boundaries of life are dispersed, and I see in what field I stand.

When on my way this afternoon, Shall I go down this long hill in the rain to fish in the pond? I ask myself. And I say to myself: Yes, roam far, grasp life and conquer it, learn much and live. Your fetters are knocked off; you are really free. Stay till late in the night; be unwise and daring. See many men far and near, in their fields and cottages before the sun sets, though as if many more were to be seen. And yet each *rencontre* shall be so satisfactory and simple that no other shall seem possible. Do not repose every night as villagers do. The noble life is continuous and unintermitting. At least, live with a longer radius. Men come home at night only from the next field or street, where their household echoes haunt, and their life pines and is sickly because it breathes its own breath. Their shadows morning and evening reach farther than their daily steps. But come home from far, from ventures and perils, from enterprise and discovery and crusading, with faith and experience and character. Do not rest much. Dismiss prudence, fear, conformity. Remember only what is promised. Make the day light you, and the night hold a candle, though you be falling from heaven to earth "from morn to dewy eve a summer's day."

Journal
August 23, 1845

IT IS A TEST QUESTION affecting the youth of a person—Have you knowledge of the morning? Do you sympathize with that season of nature? Are you abroad early, brushing the dews aside? If the sun rises on you slumbering, if you do not hear the morning cock-crow, if you do not witness the blushes of Aurora, if you are not acquainted with Venus as the morning star, what relation have you to wisdom and purity? You have then forgotten your Creator in the days of your youth! Your shutters were darkened till noon! You rose with a sick headache! In the morning sing, as do the birds. What of those birds which should slumber on their perches till the sun was an hour high? What kind of fowl would they be and new kind of bats and owls—hedge sparrows or larks? then took a dish of tea or hot coffee before they began to sing?

Journal
July 18, 1851

HOWEVER MEAN YOUR LIFE IS, MEET IT and live it; do not shun it and call it hard names. It is not so bad as you are. It looks poorest when you are richest. The fault-finder will find faults even in paradise. Love your life, poor as it is. You may perhaps have some pleasant, thrilling, glorious hours, even in a poorhouse. The setting sun is reflected from the windows of the alms-house as brightly as from the rich man's abode; the snow melts before its door as early in the spring. I do not see but a quiet mind may live as contentedly there, and have as cheering thoughts, as in a palace.

Walden, Conclusion

DO A LITTLE MORE OF THAT WORK which you have sometime con-
fessed to be good, which you feel that society and your justest
judge rightly demands of you. Do what you reprove yourself for
not doing. Know that you are neither satisfied nor dissatisfied
with yourself without reason. Let me say to you and to myself
in one breath, Cultivate the tree which you have found to bear
fruit in your soil. Regard not your past failures nor successes.
All the past is equally a failure and a success; it is a success in
as much as it offers you the present opportunity. Have you not
a pretty good thinking faculty, worth more than the rarest gold
watch? Can you not pass a judgment on something? Does not
the stream still rise to its fountain-head in you? Go to the devil
and come back again. Dispose of evil. Get punished once for
all. Die, if you can. Depart. Exchange your salvation for a glass
of water. If you know of any risk to run, run it. If you don't know
of any, enjoy confidence. Do not trouble yourself to be reli-
gious; you will never get a thank-you for it. If you can drive a nail
and have any nails to drive, drive them. If you have any
experiments you would like to try, try them; now's your chance.
Do not entertain doubts, if they are not agreeable to you. Send
them to the tavern. Do not eat unless you are hungry; there's
no need of it. Do not read the newspapers. Improve every
opportunity to be melancholy. Be as melancholy as you can be,
and note the result. Rejoice with fate. As for health, consider
yourself well, and mind your business. Who knows but you are
dead already? Do not stop to be scared yet; there are more
terrible things to come, and ever to come. Men die of fright and
live of confidence. Be not simply obedient like the vegetables;
set up your own Ebenezer. Of man's "disobedience and the
fruit," etc. Do not engage to find things as you think they are.
Do what nobody can do for you. Omit to do everything else.

Journal
1850

46

A WRITER, A MAN WRITING, is the scribe of all nature; he is the corn and the grass and the atmosphere writing. It is always essential that we love to do what we are doing, do it with a heart.

Journal
September 2, 1851

THERE IS A SEASON FOR EVERYTHING, and we do not notice a given phenomenon except at that season, if, indeed, it can be called the same phenomenon at any other season. There is a time to watch the ripples on Ripple Lake, to look for arrowheads, to study the rocks and lichens, a time to walk on sandy deserts; and the observer of nature must improve these seasons as much as the farmer his. So boys fly kites and play ball or hawkie at particular times all over the State. A wise man will know what game to play today, and play it. We must not be governed by rigid rules, as by the almanac, but let the season rule us. The moods and thoughts of man are revolving just as steadily and incessantly as nature's. Nothing must be postponed. Take time by the forelock. Now or never! You must live in the present, launch yourself on every wave, find your eternity in each moment. Fools stand on their island opportunities and look toward another land. There is no other land; there is no other life but this, or the like of this. Where the good husbandman is, there is the good soil. Take any other course, and life will be a succession of regrets. Let us see vessels sailing prosperously before the wind, and not simply stranded barks. There is no world for the penitent and regretful.

Journal
April 24, 1859

CATCH THE PACE OF THE SEASONS; have leisure to attend to every phenomenon of nature, and to entertain every thought that comes to you. Let your life be a leisurely progress through the realms of nature, even in guest-quarters.

Journal
January 11, 1852

WHY SHOULD WE BE IN SUCH DESPERATE HASTE to succeed and in such desperate enterprises? If a man does not keep pace with his companions, perhaps it is because he hears a different drummer. Let him step to the music which he hears, however measured or far away. It is not important that he should mature as soon as an apple-tree or an oak. Shall he turn his spring into summer? If the condition of things which we were made for is not yet, what were any reality which we can substitute?

Walden, Conclusion

PART 2

"Consider the Beauty of the Earth"

IN WHAT BOOK IS THIS WORLD *and its beauty described? Who has plotted the steps toward the discovery of beauty?*

Journal
October 4, 1859

"The point of view of wonder and awe"

ONE AFTERNOON IN THE FALL, November 21st, I saw Fair Haven Pond with its island and meadow; between the island and the shore, a strip of perfectly smooth water in the lee of the island; and two hawks sailing over it; and something more I saw which cannot easily be described, which made me say to myself that the landscape could not be improved. I did not see how it could be improved. Yet I do not know what these things can be; I begin to see such objects only when I leave off understanding them, and afterwards remember that I did not appreciate them before. But I get no further than this. How adapted these forms and colors to our eyes, a meadow and its islands! What are these things?

Journal
February 14, 1851

I SIT IN MY BOAT ON WALDEN, playing the flute this evening, and see the perch, which I seem to have charmed, hovering around me, and the moon travelling over the bottom, which is strewn with the wrecks of the forest, and feel that nothing but the wildest imagination can conceive of the manner of life we are living. Nature is a wizard. The Concord nights are stranger than the Arabian nights.

> Journal
> May 27, 1841

WE GET ONLY TRANSIENT and partial glimpses of the beauty of the world. Standing at the right angle, we are dazzled by the colors of the rainbow in colorless ice. From the right point of view, every storm and every drop in it is a rainbow. Beauty and music are not mere traits and exceptions. They are the rule and character. It is the exception that we see and hear.

> Journal
> December 11, 1855

HOW MUCH OF BEAUTY—of color, as well as form—on which our eyes daily rest goes unperceived by us!

> Journal
> August 1, 1860

WE ARE INTERESTED in the phenomena of Nature mainly as children are, or as we are in games of chance. They are more or less exciting. Our appetite for novelty is insatiable. We do not attend to ordinary things, though they are most important, but to extraordinary ones.

> Journal
> March 19, 1859

I SEE A MAN trimming willows on the Sudbury causeway and others raking hay out of the water in the midst of all this clarity and brightness, but are they aware of the splendor of this day? The mass of mankind, who live in houses or shops, or are *bent* upon their labor out of doors, know nothing of the beautiful days which are passing about and around them. Is not such a day worthy of a hymn? It is such a day as mankind might spend in praising and glorifying nature. It might be spent as a natural sabbath, if only all men would accept the hint, devoted to unworldly thoughts. The first bright day of the fall, the earth reflector. The dog-day mists are gone; the washed earth shines; the cooler air braces man.

Journal
August 19, 1853

IT HAS COME TO THIS—that the lover of art is one, and the lover of nature another, though true art is but the expression of our love of nature. It is monstrous when one cares but little about trees but much about Corinthian columns, and yet this is exceedingly common.

Journal
October 9, 1857

IF WE WILL BE QUIET and ready enough, we shall find compensation in every disappointment. If a shower drives us for shelter to the maple grove or the trailing branches of the pine, yet in their recesses with microscopic eye we discover some new wonder in the bark, or the leaves, or the fungi at our feet. We are interested by some new resource of insect economy, or the chickadee is more than usually familiar. We can study Nature's nooks and corners then.

Journal
September 23, 1838

SURELY, ONE MAY AS PROFITABLY be soaked in the juices of a marsh for one day, as pick his way dry-shod over sand. Cold and damp—are they not as rich experience as warmth and dryness?

So is not shade as good as sunshine, night as day? Why be eagles and thrushes always, and owls and whip-poor-wills never?

Journal
June 16, 1840

NATURE DOTH THUS KINDLY HEAL every wound. By the medication of a thousand little mosses and fungi, the most unsightly objects become radiant of beauty. There seem to be two sides of this world, presented us at different times, as we see things in growth or dissolution, in life or death. For seen with the eye of the poet, as God sees them, all things are alive and beautiful;

but seen with the historical eye, or eye of the memory, they are dead and offensive. If we see Nature as pausing, immediately all mortifies and decays; but seen as progressing, she is beautiful.

Journal
March 13, 1842

ON THE SURFACE of the water amid the maples, on the Holden Wood shore where I landed, I noticed some of the most splendid iridescence or opalescence from some oily matter, where the water was smooth amid the maples, that I ever saw. It was where some sucker or other fish, perchance, had decayed. The colors are intense blue and crimson, with dull golden. The whole at first covering seven or eight inches, but broken by the ripples I have made into polygonal figures like the fragments of a most wonderfully painted mirror. These fragments drift and turn about, apparently, as stiffly on the surface as if they were as thick and strong as glass. The colors are in many places sharply defined in fine lines, making unaccountable figures, as if they were produced by a sudden crystallization. How much color or expression can reside in so thin a substance! With such accompaniments does a sucker die and mix his juices with the river. This beauty like the rainbow and sunset sky marks the spot where his body has mingled with the elements.

Journal
May 18, 1856

THAT DELICATE, WAVING, feathery dry grass which I saw yesterday is to be remembered with the autumn. The dry grasses are not dead for me. A beautiful form has as much life at one season as another.

Journal
November 11, 1850

THE UNIVERSE IS NOT rough-hewn, but perfect in its details. Nature will bear the closest inspection; she invites us to lay our eye level with the smallest leaf, and take an insect view of its plain. She has no interstices; every part is full of life.

"Natural History"

WHEN I DETECT A BEAUTY in any of the recesses of nature, I am reminded, by the serene and retired spirit in which it requires to be contemplated, of the inexpressible privacy of a life—how silent and unambitious it is. The beauty there is in mosses must be considered from the holiest, quietest nook.

"Natural History"

NATURE DOES NOT CAST pearls before swine. There is just as much beauty visible to us in the landscape as we are prepared to appreciate—not a grain more.

"Autumnal Tints"

AS IT IS IMPORTANT TO CONSIDER Nature from the point of view of science, remembering the nomenclature and system of men, and so, if possible, go a step further in that direction, so it is equally important often to ignore or forget all that men presume that they know, and take an original and unprejudiced view of Nature, letting her make what impression she will on you, as the first men, and all children and natural men still do.

Journal
February 28, 1860

ALL THINGS IN THIS WORLD MUST be seen with the morning dew on them, must be seen with youthful, early-opened, hopeful eyes.

Journal
June 13, 1852

ALL THE PHENOMENA of nature need to be seen from the point of view of wonder and awe.

Journal
June 27, 1852

"The blood
of the
earth"

WE BETRAY OUR vegetable and animal nature and sympathies by our delight in water. We rejoice in the full rills, the melting snow, the copious spring rains and the freshets, as if we were frozen earth to be thawed, or lichens and mosses, expanding and reviving under this influence.

> *Journal*
> April 4, 1859

HOW DEAD WOULD the globe seem, especially at this season, if it were not for these water surfaces! We are slow to realize water—the beauty and magic of it. It is interestingly strange to us forever. Immortal water, alive even in the superficies, restlessly heaving now and tossing me and my boat, and sparkling with life! I look round with a thrill on this bright fluctuating surface on which no man can walk, whereon is no trace of footstep, unstained as glass.

> *Journal*
> May 8, 1854

HE CANNOT BE SAID to live who does not get pure water.
Journal
July 16, 1851

THE FINEST WORKERS in stone are not copper or steel tools, but the gentle touches of air and water working at their leisure with a liberal allowance of time.
A Week, "Wednesday"

IT IS WELL TO HAVE some water in your neighborhood, to give buoyancy to and float the earth.
Walden, "Where I Lived"

THE GREEN OF THE ICE AND WATER begins to be visible about half an hour before sunset. Is it produced by the reflected blue of the sky mingling with the yellow or pink of the setting sun? What a singular element is this water! I go shaking the river from side to side at each step, as I see by its motion at the few holes.
Journal
January 20, 1859

THERE IS SOMETHING MORE than association at the bottom of the excitement which the roar of a cataract produces. It is allied to the circulation in our veins. We have a waterfall which corresponds even to Niagara somewhere within us. It is astonishing what a rush and tumult a slight inclination will produce in a swollen brook. How it proclaims its glee, its boisterousness, rushing headlong in its prodigal course as if it would exhaust itself in half an hour! How it spends itself! I would say to the orator and poet, Flow freely and *lavishly* as a brook that is full— without stint. Perchance I have stumbled upon the origin of the word "lavish." It does not hesitate to tumble down the steepest precipice and roar or tinkle as it goes, for fear it will exhaust its fountain. The impetuosity of descending water even by the slightest inclination! It seems to flow with ever increasing rapidity.
Journal
February 12, 1851

THE SUDDEN APPARITION of this dark-blue water on the surface of the earth is exciting. I must now walk where I can see the most water, as to the most living part of nature. This is the blood of the earth, and we see its blue arteries pulsing with new life now.

> *Journal*
> February 27, 1860

I NOTICED NIGHT BEFORE LAST from Fair Haven how valuable was some water by moonlight, like the river and Fair Haven Pond, though far away, reflecting the light with a faint glimmering sheen, as in the spring of the year. The water shines with an inward light like a heaven on earth. The silent depth and serenity and majesty of water! Strange that men should distinguish gold and diamonds, when these precious elements are so common. I saw a distant river by moonlight, making no noise, yet flowing, as by day, still to the sea, like melted silver reflecting the moonlight. Far away it lay encircling the earth. How far away it may look in the night, and even from a low hill how miles away down in the valley! As far off as paradise and the delectable country! There is a certain glory attends on water by night.

> *Journal*
> June 13, 1851

HOW MUCH WOULD be subtracted from the day if the water was taken away!

> *Journal*
> April 9, 1856

"The living waters"

THE WATERS HAVE STOLEN HIGHER STILL in the night around the village, bathing higher its fences and its dry withered grass stems with a dimple. See that broad, smooth vernal lake, like a painted lake. Not a breath disturbs it. The sun and warmth and smooth water and birds make it a carnival of Nature's. I am surprised when I perceive men going about their ordinary occupations. I presume that before ten o'clock at least all the villagers will have come down to the bank and looked over this bright and placid flood—the child and the man, the house-keeper and the invalid—even as the village beholds itself reflected in it. . . . I do not imagine anything going on today away from and out of sight of the waterside.

Journal
April 9, 1856

THE RIVER, NOW THAT IT IS SO CLEAR and sunny, is better than any aquarium. Standing up and pushing gently up the stream, or floating yet more quietly down it, I can, in some places, see the secrets of half the river and its inhabitants—the common and familiar bream with the dusty light reflected from its fins, the vigorous-looking perch, tiger-like among fishes (I notice that many of the perch are poised head downward, peeping under the rocks), the motionless pickerel with reticulated back and sides, as it were the seed-vessel of a water-plant, eyes set far back. It is an enchanter's wand ready to surprise you with life.

> *Journal*
> August 8, 1859

FOR THE FIRST TIME it occurred to me this afternoon what a piece of wonder a river is—a huge volume of matter ceaselessly rolling through the fields and meadows of this substantial earth, making haste from the high places, by stable dwellings of men and Egyptian Pyramids, to its restless reservoir. One would think that, by a very natural impulse, the dwellers upon the headwaters of the Mississippi and Amazon would follow in the trail of their waters to see the end of the matter.

> *Journal*
> September 5, 1838

WHAT CAN BE MORE IMPRESSIVE than to look up a noble river just at evening—one, perchance, which you have never explored—and behold its placid waters, reflecting the woods and sky, lapsing inaudibly toward the ocean; to behold as a lake, but know it as a river, tempting the beholder to explore it and his own destiny at once? Haunt of waterfowl. This was above the factories—all that I saw. That water could never have flowed under a factory. How *then* could it have reflected the sky?

> *Journal*
> July 9, 1851

WE ARE MADE TO LOVE the river and the meadow, and the wind to ripple the water.

> *Journal*
> February 14, 1851

THE RIVER, TOO, STEADILY YIELDS its crop. In louring days it is remarkable how many villagers resort to it. It is of more worth than many gardens. I meet one, late in the afternoon, going to the river with his basket on his arm and his pole in hand, not ambitious to catch pickerel this time, but he thinks he may perhaps get a mess of small fish. These kind of values are real and important, though but little appreciated, and he is not a wise legislator who underrates them and allows the bridges to be built low so as to prevent the passage of small boats. The town is but little conscious how much interest it has in the river, and might vote it away any day thoughtlessly.

Journal
July 20, 1851

THE REACH OF THE RIVER between Bedford and Carlisle, seen from a distance in the road today, as formerly, has a singularly ethereal, celestial, or elysian look. It is of a light sky-blue, alternating with smoother white streaks, where the surface reflects the light differently, like a milk-pan full of the milk of Valhalla partially skimmed, more gloriously and heavenly fair and pure than the sky itself. It is something more celestial than the sky above it. . . . We have names for the rivers of hell, but none for the rivers of heaven, unless the Milky Way be one. It is such a smooth and shining blue, like a panoply of sky-blue plates. . . . Such water as that river reach appears to me of quite incalculable value, and the man who would blot that out of his prospect for a sum of money does not otherwise than to sell heaven.

Journal
October 6, 1851

HOW PERFECTLY NEW and fresh the world is seen to be, when we behold a myriad sparkles of brilliant white sunlight on a rippled stream! So remote from dust and decay, more bright than the flash of an eye.

Journal
May 24, 1860

RIVERS MUST HAVE BEEN the guides which conducted the footsteps of the first travellers. They are the constant lure, when they flow by our doors, to distant enterprise and adventure; and, by a natural impulse, the dwellers on their banks will at length accompany their currents to the lowlands of the globe, or explore at their invitation the interior of continents. They are the natural highways of all nations, not only levelling the ground and removing obstacles from the path of the traveller, quenching his thirst, and bearing him on their bosoms, but conducting him through the most interesting scenery, the most populous portions of the globe, and where the animal and vegetable kingdoms attain the greatest perfection.

A Week, "Concord River"

THE RIVER IS MY OWN HIGHWAY, the only wild and unfenced part of the world hereabouts.

Journal
May 30, 1852

OTHER ROADS DO SOME violence to Nature, and bring the traveller to stare at her, but the river steals into the scenery it traverses without intrusion, silently creating and adorning it, and is as free to come and go as the zephyr.

A Week, "Wednesday"

WITHOUT BEING THE OWNER of any land, I find that I have a civil right in the river—that, if I am not a land-owner I am a water-owner. It is fitting, therefore, that I should have a boat, a cart, for this my farm. Since it is almost wholly given up to a few of us, while the other highways are much travelled, no wonder that I improve it. Such a one as I will choose to dwell in a township where there are most ponds and rivers and our range is widest. In relation to the river, I find my natural rights least infringed on. It is an extensive "common" still left.

Journal
March 23, 1853

I THINK THAT I SPEAK IMPARTIALLY when I say that I have never met with a stream so suitable for boating and botanizing as the Concord, and fortunately nobody knows it. I know of reaches which a single country-seat would spoil beyond remedy, but there has not been any important change here since I can remember. The willows slumber along its shore, piled in light but low masses, even like the cumuli clouds above. We pass haymakers in every meadow, who may think that we are idlers. But Nature takes care that every nook and crevice is explored by some one. While they look after the open meadows, we farm the tract between the river's brinks and behold the shores from that side.

Journal
August 6, 1858

HOW MANY MEMORABLE localities in a river walk! Here is the warm wood-side; next, the good fishing bay; and next, where the old settler was drowned when crossing on the ice a hundred years ago. It is all storied.

Journal
January 27, 1860

I CANNOT HELP BEING encouraged by this blithe activity in the elements in these degenerate days of men. Who hears the rippling of the rivers will not utterly despair of anything.

Journal
December 12, 1841

NOT A FISH CAN LEAP or an insect fall on the pond but it is thus reported in circling dimples, in lines of beauty, as it were the constant welling up of its fountain, the gentle pulsing of its life, the heaving of its breast. . . . How peaceful the phenomena of the lake!

Walden, "The Ponds"

THE MAN MUST NOT drink of the running streams, the living waters, who is not prepared to have all nature reborn in him—to suckle monsters.

Journal
August 17, 1851

[This statement seemed exaggerated, overly emphatic even for Henry, until I drank of the wrong living waters and suckled monsters. My particular monster was the Mini Watu—what Sioux Indians call water imps. What modern medicine calls Giardia. I was not at all prepared for these parasites to set up their little shop of protozoan horrors in my stomach. Like a batch of explosive powdermilk biscuits, they will make you, shy or not, jump up and do what must be done. When these imps strike in public, they will make you panic and run like you had a monster in close pursuit. I now prepare so that I will never have this particular nature reborn in me again.]

"The circle
of the
seasons"

I WANT TO GO SOON and live away by the pond, where I shall hear only the wind whispering among the reeds. It will be success if I shall have left myself behind. But my friends ask what I will do when I get there. Will it not be employment enough to watch the progress of the seasons?

Journal
December 24, 1841

THIS IS JUNE, THE MONTH OF grass and leaves. The deciduous trees are investing the evergreens and revealing how dark they are. Already the aspens are trembling again, and a new summer is offered me. I feel a little fluttered in my thoughts, as if I might be too late. Each season is but an infinitesimal point. It no sooner comes than it is gone. It has no duration. It simply gives a tone and hue to my thought. Each annual phenomenon is a reminiscence and prompting. Our thoughts and sentiments answer to the revolutions of the seasons, as two cogwheels fit into each other. We are conversant with only one point of contact at a time, from which we receive a prompting and impulse and instantly pass to a new season or point of contact. A year is made up of a certain series and number of sensations and thoughts which have their language in nature. Now I am ice, now I am sorrel. Each experience reduces itself to a mood of the mind.

Journal
June 6, 1857

AS A CHILD LOOKS forward to the coming of the summer, so could we contemplate with quiet joy the circle of the seasons returning without fail eternally.

Journal
January 6, 1838

EACH NEW YEAR IS a surprise to us. We find that we had virtually forgotten the note of each bird, and when we hear it again it is remembered like a dream, reminding us of a previous state of existence. How happens it that the associations it awakens are always pleasing, never saddening; reminiscences of our sanest hours?

Journal
March 18, 1858

THE CHANGE FROM STORM and winter to serene and mild weather, from the dark and sluggish hours to bright and elastic ones, is a memorable crisis which all things proclaim.

Walden, "Spring"

HEARD TWO HAWKS SCREAM. There was something truly March-like in it, like a prolonged blast or whistling of the wind through a crevice in the sky, which, like a cracked blue saucer, overlaps the woods. Such are the first rude notes which prelude the summer's choir, learned of the whistling March wind.

Journal
March 2, 1855

AH! I HAVE PENETRATED TO those meadows on the morning of many a first spring day, jumping from hummock to hummock, from willow root to willow root, when the wild river valley and the woods were bathed in so pure and bright a light as would have waked the dead, if they had been slumbering in their graves, as some suppose.

Walden, "Spring"

THE FIRST SPARROW OF SPRING! The year beginning with younger hope than ever! The faint silvery warblings heard over the partially bare and moist fields from the blue-bird, the song-sparrow, and the red-wing, as if the last flakes of winter tinkled as they fell! What at such a time are histories, chronologies, traditions, and all written revelations? The brooks sing carols and glees to the spring. The marsh-hawk, sailing low over the meadow is already seeking the first slimy life that awakes. The sinking sound of melting snow is heard in all dells, and the ice dissolves apace in the ponds. The grass flames up on the hillsides like a spring fire.

Walden, "Spring"

IN A PLEASANT SPRING MORNING all men's sins are forgiven. You may have known your neighbor yesterday for a drunkard and a thief, and merely pitied or despised him, and despaired of the world; but the sun shines bright and warm this first spring morning, and you meet him quietly, serenely at any work, and see how even his exhausted, debauched veins and nerves expand with still joy and bless the new day, feel the spring influence with the innocence. . . .

Journal
1850

THERE IS, AT ANY RATE, such a phenomenon as the willows shining in the spring sun, however it is to be accounted for.

Journal
March 16, 1856

I THOUGHT THE OTHER DAY, How we enjoy a warm and pleasant day at this season! We dance like gnats in the sun.

Journal
March 25, 1859

SOME FIELDS ARE DRIED sufficiently for the games of ball with which this season is commonly ushered in. I associate this day, when I can remember it, with games of baseball played over behind the hills in the russet fields toward Sleepy Hollow, where the snow was just melted and dried up, . . .

Journal
April 10, 1856

THE TUPELO SHOWS SIGNS of life, but is later than the black willow; not so late, nearly, as the button-bush. The oaks are in the gray. Some in warm localities already have expanded small leaves, both black, red, and shrub oak. The large light-yellowish scales of the hickory buds, also, are turned back, revealing blossom-buds and little clusters of tender leaves ready to unfold, and the new web of verdure is spreading thick and palpable over the forest. Shade is being born; the summer is pitching its tent; concealment will soon be afforded to the birds in which to build their nests.

Journal
May 12, 1853

NOW BEGINS THE SLIGHTLY sultryish morning air into which you awake early to hear the faint buzz of a fly or hum of other insect. The teeming air, deep and hollow, filled with some spiritus, pregnant as not in winter or spring, with room for imps—good angels and bad—many chambers in it, infinite sounds. I partially awake the first time for a month at least. As if the cope of the sky lifted, the heat stretched and swelled it as a bladder, and it remained permanently higher and more infinite for the summer.

Journal
May 22, 1854

A HOT MIDSUMMER DAY with a sultry mistiness in the air and shadows on land and water beginning to have a peculiar distinctness and solidity. The river, smooth and still, with a deepened shade of the elms on it, like midnight suddenly revealed, its bed-curtains shoved aside, has a sultry languid look. The atmosphere now imparts a bluish or glaucous tinge to the distant trees.

Journal
July 18, 1854

ASTERS AND GOLDEN-RODS were the livery which nature wore at present. The latter alone expressed all the ripeness of the season, and shed their mellow lustre over the fields, as if the now declining summer's sun had bequeathed its hues to them. It is the floral solstice a little after mid summer, when the particles of golden light, the sun-dust, have, as it were, fallen like seeds on the earth, and produced these blossoms. On every hill side, and in every valley, stood countless asters, coreopses, tansies, golden-rods, and the whole race of yellow flowers.

A Week, "Friday"

AS WE LAY AWAKE long before day break, listening to the rippling of the river and the rustling of the leaves, in suspense whether the wind blew up or down the stream, was favorable or unfavorable to our voyage, we already suspected that there was a change in the weather, from a freshness as of autumn in these sounds. The wind in the woods sounded like an incessant waterfall dashing and roaring amid rocks, and we even felt encouraged by the unusual activity of the elements. He who hears the rippling of rivers in these degenerate days will not utterly despair. That night was the turning-point in the season. We had gone to bed in summer, and we awoke in autumn; for summer passes into autumn in some unimaginable point of time, like the turning of a leaf.

A Week, "Friday"

WE SOON PASSED the mouth of the Souhegan, and the village of Merrimack, and as the mist gradually rolled away, and we were relieved from the trouble of watching for rocks, we saw by the flitting clouds, by the first russet tinge on the hills, by the rushing river, the cottages on shore, and the shore itself, so coolly fresh and shining with dew, and later in the day, by the hue of the grape-vine, the goldfinch on the willow, the flickers flying in flocks, and when we passed near enough to the shore, as we fancied, by the faces of men, that the Fall had commenced.

A *Week*, "Friday"

SOME SINGLE RED MAPLES are very splendid now, the whole tree bright-scarlet against the cold green pines; now, when very few trees are changed, a most remarkable object in the landscape; seen a mile off. It is too fair to be believed, especially seen against the light. Some are a reddish or else greenish yellow, others with red or yellow cheeks.

Journal
September 26, 1854

THE TEN DAYS—at least—before this were plainly Indian summer. They were remarkably pleasant and warm. The latter half I sat and slept with an open window, though the first part of the time I had a little fire in the morning. These succeeded to days when you had worn thick clothing and sat by fires for some time.

Journal
October 15, 1857

THE BRILLIANT AUTUMNAL COLORS are red and yellow and the various tints, hues, and shades of these. Blue is reserved to be the color of the sky, but yellow and red are the colors of the earth flower. Every fruit, on ripening, and just before its fall, acquires a bright tint. So do the leaves; so the sky before the end of the day, and the year near its setting. October is the red sunset sky, November the later twilight. Color stands for all ripeness and success.

Journal
October 24, 1858

71

I DO NOT SEE WHY, since America and her autumn woods have been discovered, our leaves should not compete with the precious stones in giving names to colors; and, indeed, I believe that in course of time the names of some of our trees and shrubs, as well as flowers, will get into our popular chromatic nomenclature.

But of much more importance than a knowledge of the names and distinctions of color is the joy and exhilaration which these colored leaves excite. Already these brilliant trees throughout the street, without any more variety, are at least equal to an annual festival and holiday, or a week of such. These are cheap and innocent gala-days, celebrated by one and all without the aid of committees or marshals, such a show as may safely be licensed, not attracting gamblers or rum-sellers, not requiring any special police to keep the peace. And poor indeed must be that New-England village's October which has not the Maple in its streets. This October festival costs no powder, nor ringing of bells, but every tree is a living liberty-pole on which a thousand bright flags are waving.

"Autumnal Tints"

WHY DO YOU FLEE so soon, sir, to the theatres, lecture-rooms, and museums of the city? If you will stay here awhile I will promise you strange sights. You shall walk on water; all these brooks and rivers and ponds shall be your highway. You shall see the whole earth covered a foot or more deep with purest white crystals, in which you slump or over which you glide, and all the trees and stubble glittering in icy armor.

Journal
October 18, 1859

A GRAY, OVERCAST, STILL day, and more small birds—tree sparrows and chickadees—than usual about the house. There have been a very few fine snowflakes falling for many hours, and now, by 2 P.M., a regular snow-storm has commenced, fine flakes falling steadily, and rapidly whitening all the landscape.

In half an hour the russet earth is painted white even to the horizon. Do we know of any other so silent and sudden a change?

Journal
November 28, 1858

WHAT A WORLD WE LIVE IN! WHERE myriads of these little disks, so beautiful to the most prying eye, are whirled down on every traveller's coat, the observant and the unobservant, and on the restless squirrel's fur, and on the far-stretching fields and forests, the wooded dells, and the mountain-tops. Far, far away from the haunts of man, they roll down some little slope, fall over and come to their bearings, and melt or lose their beauty in the mass, ready anon to swell some little rill with their contribution, and so, at last, the universal ocean from which they came. There they lie, like the wreck of chariot-wheels after a battle in the skies. Meanwhile the meadow mouse shoves them aside in his gallery, the schoolboy casts them in his snowball, or the woodman's sled glides smoothly over them, these glorious spangles, the sweeping of heaven's floor.

Journal
January 5, 1856

WE ARE RAINED AND SNOWED ON with gems. I confess that I was a little encouraged, for I was beginning to believe that Nature was poor and mean, and I was now convinced that she turned off as good work as ever. What a world we live in! Where are the jewellers' shops? There is nothing handsomer than a snow-flake and a dewdrop. I may say that the maker of the world exhausts his skill with each snowflake and dewdrop that he sends down.

Journal
January 6, 1858

"The voice
of nature"

DEBAUCHED AND WORN-OUT senses require the violent vibrations of an instrument to excite them, but *sound* and still youthful senses, not enervated by luxury, hear music in the wind and rain and running water. One would think from reading the critics that music was intermittent as a spring in the desert, depending on some Paganini or Mozart, or heard only when the Pierians or Euterpeans drive through the villages; but music is perpetual, and only hearing is intermittent.

Journal
February 8, 1857

THE WIND IN THE WOOD yonder sounds like an incessant waterfall, the water dashing and roaring among rocks.

Journal
December 12, 1841

THE FIRST PARTRIDGE drums in one or two places, as if the earth's pulse now beat audibly with the increased flow of life. It slightly flutters all Nature and makes her heart palpitate. Also, as I stand listening for the wren, and sweltering in my great-coat, I hear the woods filled with the hum of insects, as if my hearing were affected; and thus the summer's choir begins. The silent spaces have begun to be filled with notes of birds and insects and the peep and croak and snore of frogs, even as living green blades are everywhere pushing up amid the sere ones.

Journal
April 25, 1854

[*The old-world term "partridge," occasionally still used, especially in rural areas and restaurants, was applied to North American grouse, chickens and hens by early settlers. The partridge Thoreau often saw or heard drumming was the ruffed grouse.*]

THE SOUND OF THE CRICKETS at dawn after these first sultry nights seems like the dreaming of the earth still continued into the daylight. I love that early twilight hour when the crickets still creak right on with such dewy faith and promise, as if it were still night—expressing the innocence of morning—when the creak of the cricket is fresh and bedewed.... The earth-song of the cricket! Before Christianity was, it is. Health! health! health! is the burden of its song.

Journal
June 17, 1852

I WONDER THAT WILD MEN have not made more of echoes, or that we do not hear that they have made more. It would be a pleasant, a soothing and cheerful mission to go about the country in search of them—articulating, speaking, vocal, oracular, resounding, sonorous, hollow, prophetic places; places wherein to found an oracle, sites for oracles, sacred ears of Nature.

Journal
1850

WE WERE NOT SO LUCKY as to hear wolves howl, though that is an occasional serenade. Some friends of mine, who two years ago went up the Caucomgomoc River, were serenaded by wolves while moose-hunting by moonlight.

The Maine Woods, "Allegash"

[*This quote is a shorter version of the same selection found in the category "A wild creature."*]

FAR BELOW US WAS the beach, from half a dozen to a dozen rods in width, with a long line of breakers rushing to the strand. The sea was exceedingly dark and stormy, the sky completely overcast, the clouds still dropping rain, and the wind seemed to blow not so much as the exciting cause, as from sympathy with the already agitated ocean. The waves broke on the bars at some distance from the shore, and curving green or yellow as if over so many unseen dams, ten or twelve feet high, like a thousand waterfalls, rolled in foam to the sand.

Cape Cod, "The Beach"

AS WE LAY HUDDLED TOGETHER under the tent, which leaked considerably about the sides, with our baggage at our feet, we listened to some of the grandest thunder which I ever heard— rapid peals, round and plump, bang, bang, bang, in succession, like artillery from some fortress in the sky; and the lightning was proportionally brilliant.

The Maine Woods, "Allegash"

IT WAS MYTHOLOGIC, and an Indian might have referred it to a departed spirit. The fiddles made by the trees whose limbs cross one another—played on by the wind!

Journal
April 9, 1859

THE FOREST HAS LOST so many leaves that its floor and paths are much more checkered with light. I hear no sound but the rustling of the withered leaves, which lulls the few and silent birds to sleep, and, on the wooded hilltops, the roar of the wind. Each tree is a harp which resounds all night, though some have but a few leaves left to flutter and hum.

Journal
October 28, 1852

BEYOND THIS WE BY GOOD LUCK fell into another path, and following this or a branch of it, at our discretion, through a forest consisting of large white pines—the first we had seen in our walk—we at length heard the roar of falling water, and came out at the head of the Falls of St. Anne.

"A Yankee in Canada"
(St. Anne)

THE GROUND IS SONOROUS, like seasoned wood, and even the ordinary rural sounds are melodious, and the jingling of the ice on the trees is sweet and liquid.

"A Winter Walk"

THE VOICE OF NATURE is always encouraging.

Journal
March 18, 1858

"Sweet wild birds"

ONLY THINK HOW FINELY our life is furnished in all its details—sweet wild birds provided to fill its interstices with song! It is provided that while we are employed in our corporeal, or intellectual, or other, exercises we shall be lulled and amused or cheered by the singing of birds. When the laborer rests on his spade today, the sun having just come out, he is not left wholly to the mercy of this thoughts, nature is not a mere void to him, but he can hardly fail to hear the pleasing and encouraging notes of some newly arrived bird. The strain of the grass finch is very likely to fall on his ear and convince him, whether he is conscious of it or not, that the world is beautiful and life a fair enterprise to engage in. It will make him calm and contented. If you yield for a moment to the impressions of sense, you hear some bird giving expression to its happiness in a pleasant strain. We are provided with singing birds and with ears to hear them. What an institution that! Nor are we obliged to catch and cage them, nor to be bird-fanciers in the common sense. Whether a man's work be hard or easy, whether he be happy or unhappy, a bird is appointed to sing to a man while he is at his work.

Journal
April 15, 1859

[*Grass finch was a former common name for the vesper sparrow.*]

WHILE DROPPING BEANS in the garden at Texas just after sundown (May 13th), I hear from across the fields the note of the bay-wing, *Come here here there there quick quick quick or I'm gone* (which I have no doubt sits on some fence-post or rail there), and it instantly translates me from the sphere of my work and repairs all the world that we jointly inhabit. It reminds me of so many country afternoons and evenings when this bird's strain was heard far over the fields, as I pursued it from field to field. The spirit of its earth-song, of its serene and true philosophy, was breathed into me, and I saw the world as through a glass, as it lies eternally. Some of its aboriginal contentment, even of its domestic felicity, possessed me. What he suggests is permanently true. As the bay-wing sang many a thousand years ago, so sang he tonight.

Journal
May 12, 1857

[*Bay-wing was another former common name for the vesper sparrow.*]

I HEAR FAINTLY THE CAWING of a crow far, far away, echoing from some unseen wood-side, as if deadened by the springlike vapor which the sun is drawing from the ground. It mingles with the slight murmur of the village, the sound of children at play, as one stream empties gently into another, and the wild and tame are one. What a delicious sound! It is not merely crow calling to crow, for it speaks to me too. I am part of one great creature with him; if he has voice, I have ears. I can hear when he calls, and have engaged not to shoot nor stone him if he will caw to me each spring.

Journal
January 12, 1855

THERE ARE FEW, IF ANY, so coarse and insensible that they are not interested to hear that the bluebird has come. The Irish laborer has learned to distinguish him and report his arrival. It is a part of the news of the season to the lawyer in his office and the mechanic in his shop, as well as to the farmer. One will remember, perchance, to tell you that he saw one a week ago in the next town or county. Citizens just come into the country to live put up a bluebird box, and record in some kind of journal the date of the first arrival observed—though it may be rather a late one. The farmer can tell you when he saw the first one, if you ask him within a week.

Journal
March 7, 1859

A MAN'S INTEREST in a single bluebird is worth more than a complete but dry list of the fauna and flora of a town.

Letter to Daniel Ricketson
November 22, 1858

STANDING THERE, THOUGH in this *bare* November landscape, I am reminded of the incredible phenomenon of small birds in winter—that ere long, amid the cold powdery snow, as it were a fruit of the season, will come twittering a flock of delicate crimson-tinged birds, lesser redpolls, to sport and feed on the seeds and buds now just ripe for them on the sunny side of a wood, shaking down the powdery snow there in their cheerful social feeding, as if it were high midsummer to them. These crimson aerial creatures have wings which would bear them quickly to the regions of summer, but here is all the summer they want. What a rich contrast! tropical colors, crimson breasts, on cold white snow! Such etherealness, such delicacy in their forms, such ripeness in their colors, in this stern and barren season! It is as surprising as if you were to find a brilliant crimson flower which flourished amid snows. They greet the chopper and the hunter in their furs.

Journal
December 11, 1855

How MANY LITTLE BIRDS of the warbler family are busy now about the opening buds, while I sit by the spring! They are almost as much a part of the tree as its blossoms and leaves. They come and give it voice.

Journal
May 11, 1853

AT THE SAME TIME I caught sight of a bird with a very conspicuous deep-orange throat and otherwise dark, with some streaks along the head. This may have been the Blackburnian warbler, if it was not too large for that, and may have been the singer.

Journal
June 4, 1858

You MUST ATTEND to the birds in the spring.

Journal
June 11, 1852

A CHILD ASKED concerning a bobolink, "What makes he sing so sweet, Mother? Do he eat flowers?"

Journal
June 20, 1857

THE SONOROUS, QUAVERING sounds of the geese are the voice of this cloudy air—a sound that comes from directly between us and the sky, an aerial sound, and yet so distinct, heavy, and sonorous, a clanking chain drawn through the heavy air. I saw through my window some children looking up and pointing their tiny bows into the heavens, and I knew at once that the geese were in the air. It is always an exciting event. The children, instinctively aware of its importance, rushed into the house to tell their parents.

Journal
November 8, 1857

WOULD IT NOT BE WELL to carry a spy-glass in order to watch these shy birds such as ducks and hawks? In some respects, methinks, it would be better than a gun. The latter brings them nearer dead, but the former alive. You can identify the species better by killing the bird, because it was a dead specimen that was so minutely described, but you can study the habits and appearance best in the living specimen.

Journal
March 29, 1853

I SAW A PIGEON-PLACE on George Heywood's cleared lot, with the six dead trees set up for the pigeons to alight on, and the brush-house close by to conceal the man. I was rather startled to find such a thing going now in Concord. The pigeons on the trees looked like fabulous birds, with their long tails and their pointed breasts. I could hardly believe they were alive and not some wooden birds used for decoys, they sat so still, and even when they moved their necks I thought it was the effect of art.

"Days and Nights in Concord"

[In Memoriam:

The pigeon Thoreau refers to is the extinct passenger pigeon. Especially graceful and elegant, the passenger pigeon—long-tailed and 15 to 18 inches in length—was a beautifully colored bird that flew straight and fast as a duck. Its iridescent neck feathers glowed in the sun.

The relentless slaughter of market hunting (live decoys were called "stool pigeons"), combined with the cutting of the hardwood forests in the eastern United States, extinguished them in an amazingly short time. In 1914 the last passenger pigeon—a bird born in captivity named Martha— died mateless, cagebound, oblivious to the fate of her species, at the Cincinnati Zoo. And with her death, the most numerous bird (billions) on earth just 150 years before, was gone.]

HE WHO CUTS DOWN WOODS beyond a certain limit exterminates birds.

Journal
May 17, 1853

WHAT IS AN EAGLE in captivity—screaming in a courtyard! I am not the wiser respecting eagles for having seen one there.

Journal
March 15, 1860

SAW A LARGE BIRD SAIL ALONG over the edge of Wheeler's cranberry meadow just below Fair Haven, which I at first thought a gull, but with my glass found it was a hawk and had a perfectly white head and tail and broad or blackish wings. It sailed and circled along over the low cliff, and the crows dived at it in the field of my glass, and I saw it well, both above and beneath, as it turned, and then it passed off to hover over the Cliffs at a greater height. It was undoubtedly a white-headed eagle.

Journal
April 8, 1854

METHINKS THE HAWK that soars so loftily and circles so steadily and apparently without effort has earned this power by faithfully creeping on the ground as a reptile in a former state of existence.

Journal
November 12, 1851

ALL THAT WAS RIPEST and fairest in the wilderness and the wild man is preserved and transmitted to us in the strain of the wood thrush.

Journal
June 22, 1853

THE THRUSH ALONE declares the immortal wealth and vigor that is in the forest.

Journal
July 5, 1852

I REJOICE THAT THERE are owls. They represent the stark, twilight, unsatisfied thoughts I have. Let owls do the idiotic and maniacal hooting for men. This sound faintly suggests the infinite roominess of nature, that there is a world in which owls live.

Journal
November 18, 1851

ON THE 29TH OF APRIL, as I was fishing from the bank of the river near the Nine-Acre-Corner bridge, standing on the quaking grass and willow roots, where the muskrats lurk, I heard a singular rattling sound, somewhat like that of the sticks which

83

boys play with their fingers, when, looking up, I observed a very slight and graceful hawk, like a night-hawk, alternately soaring like a ripple and tumbling a rod or two over and over, showing the underside of its wings, which gleamed like a satin ribbon in the sun, or like the pearly inside of a shell. This sight reminded me of falconry and what nobleness and poetry are associated with that sport. The merlin it seemed to me it might be called: but I care not for its name. It was the most ethereal flight I had ever witnessed. It did not simply flutter like a butterfly, nor soar like the larger hawks, but it sported with proud reliance in the fields of air; mounting again and again with its strange chuckle, it repeated its free and beautiful fall, turning over and over like a kite, and then recovering from its lofty tumbling, as if it had never set its foot on *terra firma*. It appeared to have no companion in the universe—sporting there alone—and to need none but the morning and the ether with which it played. It was not lonely, but made all the earth lonely beneath it. Where was the parent which hatched it, its kindred, and its father in the heavens? The tenant of the air, it seemed related to the earth but by an egg hatched some time in the crevice of a crag—or was its native nest made in the angle of a cloud, woven of the rainbow's trimmings and the sunset sky, and lined with some soft midsummer haze caught up from earth? Its eyry now some cliffy cloud.

Walden, "Spring"

Saw a tanager in Sleepy Hollow. It most takes the eye of any bird. You here have the red-wing reversed—the deepest scarlet of the red-wing spread over the whole body, not on the wing-coverts merely, while the wings are black. It flies through the green foliage as if it would ignite the leaves.

Journal
May 20, 1853

At Loring's Wood heard and saw a tanager. That contrast of a *red* bird with the green pines and the blue sky! Even when I have heard his note and look for him and find the bloody fellow, sitting on a dead twig of a pine, I am always startled. That incredible red, with the green and blue, as if these were the trinity we wanted. . . . I am transported; these are not the woods I ordinarily walk in. . . . How he enhances the wildness and wealth of the woods!

Journal
May 23, 1853

THE RED-WING'S *o'gurgle-ee-e* is in singular harmony with the sound and impression of the lapsing stream or the smooth, swelling flood beneath his perch. He gives expression to the flood. The water reaches far in amid the trees on which he sits, and they seem like a water-organ played on by the flood. The sound rises up through their pipes.

Journal
April 9, 1856

I SEE SOME FEATHERS of a blue jay scattered along a wood-path, and at length come to the body of the bird. What a neat and delicately ornamented creature, finer than any work of art in a lady's boudoir, with its soft light purplish-blue crest and its dark-blue or purplish secondaries (the narrow half) finely barred with dusky. It is the more glorious to live in Concord because the jay is so splendidly painted.

Journal
November 13, 1858

MEANWHILE I HEAR a loud hum and see a splendid male hummingbird coming zigzag in long tacks, like a bee, but far swifter, along the edge of the swamp, in hot haste. He turns aside to taste the honey of the *Andromeda* within a rod of me. This golden-green gem. Its burnished back looks as if covered with green scales dusted with gold. It hovers, as it were stationary in the air, with an intense humming before each little flower-bell of the humble *Andromeda*, and inserts its long tongue in each, turning toward me that splendid ruby on its breast, that glowing ruby.

Journal
May 17, 1856

SAW IN THE POOL at the Hemlocks what I at first thought was a brighter leaf moved by the zephyr on the surface of the smooth dark water, but it was a splendid male summer duck, which allowed us to approach within seven or eight rods, sailing up close to the shore, and then rose and flew up the curving stream. We soon overhauled it again, and got a fair and long view of it. It was a splendid bird, a perfect floating gem, and Blake, who had never seen the like, was greatly surprised, not knowing that so splendid a bird was found in this part of the world. There it was, constantly moving back and forth by invisible means and wheeling on the smooth surface, showing now its breast, now its side, now its rear. It had a large, rich, flowing, green burnished crest—a most ample head-dress—two crescents of dazzling white on the side of the head and the black neck, a pinkish(?)-red bill (with black tip) and similar irides, and a long white mark under and at wing point on sides; the side, as if the form of wing at this distance, light bronze or greenish brown; but, above all, its breast, when it turns into the right light, all aglow with splendid purple (?) or ruby (?) reflections, *like the throat of the hummingbird*. It might not appear so close at hand. This was the most surprising to me. What an ornament to a river to see that glowing gem floating in contact with its waters!

Journal
November 9, 1855

[*Before the advent of bird guides, wood ducks were often called summer ducks.*]

I SEE DUCKS or teal flying silent, swift, and straight, the wild creatures.

Journal
September 20, 1851

A FLIGHT OF DUCKS adds to the wildness of our wildest river scenery.

Journal
April 17, 1852

I THINK IT MUST BE a grosbeak. At first I thought I saw a chewink, as it sat within a rod sideways to me, and I was going to call Sophia to look at it, but then it turned its breast full toward me and I saw the blood-red breast, a *large* triangular painted spot occupying the greater part of the breast. It was in the cool, shaded underwood by the old path just under the Cliff. It is a memorable event to meet with so rare a bird. Birds answer to flowers, both in their abundance and their rareness. The meeting with a rare and beautiful bird like this is like meeting with some rare and beautiful flower, which you may never find again, perchance, like the great purple fringed orchis, at least. How much it enhances the wildness and the richness of the forest to see in it some beautiful bird which you never detected before!

Journal
June 13, 1853

JOHN GARFIELD BROUGHT ME this morning (September 6th) a young great heron, which he shot this morning on a pine tree on the North Branch. It measured four feet, nine inches, from bill to toe and six feet in alar extent, and belongs to a different race from myself and Mr. Frost. I am glad to recognize him for a native of America—why not an American citizen?

Journal
August 31, 1850

"A *wild* creature"

I AM READING WILLIAM WOOD'S "New England's Prospect." He left New England August 15th, 1633, and the last English edition referred to in this American one of 1764 is that of London, 1639. . . .

Of quadrupeds no longer found in Concord, he names the lion—that Cape Ann Lion "which some affirm that they have seen," which may have been a cougar, for he adds, "Plimouth men have traded for Lions skins in former times"—bear, moose, deer, porcupines, "the grim-fac'd Ounce, and rav'nous howling Wolf," and beaver. Martens.

"For Bears they be common, being a black kind of Bear, which be most fierce in strawberry time, at which time they have young ones; at which time likewise they will go upright like a man, and climb trees, and swim to the islands;" etc. In the winter they lie in "the clifts of rocks and thick swamps." The wolves hunt these in packs and "tear him as a Dog will tear a Kid." "They never prey upon the English cattle, or offer to assault the person of any man," unless shot. Their meat "esteemed . . . above venison."

For moose and deer see Indian book.

Complains of the wolf as the great devourer of bear, moose, and deer, which kept them from multiplying more. "Of these Deer there be a great many, and more in the Massachusetts-Bay, than in any other place." "Some have killed sixteen Deer in a day upon this island," so called because the deer swam thither to avoid the wolves.

For porcupine and racoon *vide* Indian book.

Gray squirrels were evidently more numerous than now.

I do not know whether his ounce or wild cat is the Canada lynx or wolverine. He calls it wild cat and does not describe the little wildcat. Says they are accounted "very good meat. Their skins be a very deep kind of fur, spotted white and black on the belly." Audubon and Bachman make the *Lynx rufus* black and white beneath. For wolf *vide* Indian book. He says: "These be killed daily in some places or other. . . . Yet is there little hope of their utter destruction." "Travelling in the swamp by kennels."

Says the beaver are so cunning the English "seldom or never kill any of them, being not patient to lay a long siege" and not having experience.

Eagles are probably less common; pigeons of course; heath cocks all gone (price "four pence"); and turkeys (good cock, "four shillings"). Probably more owls then, and cormorants, etc., etc., sea-fowl generally and swans. Of pigeons, "Many of them build among the pine trees, thirty miles to the north-east of our plantations; joining nest to nest, and tree to tree by their nests, so that the Sun never sees the ground in that place, from whence the Indians fetch whole loads of them." And then for turkeys, tracking them in winter, or shooting them on their roosts at night. Of the crane, "almost as tall as a man," probably blue heron—possibly the whooping crane or else the sandhill—he says, "I have seen many of these fowls, yet did I never see one that was fat, though very sleaky;" neither did I. "There be likewise many Swans, which frequent the fresh ponds and rivers, seldom consorting themselves with ducks and geese; these be very good meat, the price of one is six shillings." Think of that! They had not only brant and common

gray wild geese, but "a white Goose," probably the snow goose; "sometimes there will be two or three thousand in a flock;" continue six weeks after Michaelmas and return again north in March. Peabody says of the snow goose, "They are occasionally seen in Massachusetts Bay."

Sturgeon were taken at Cape Cod and in the Merrimack especially, "pickled and brought to England, some of these be 12, 14, and 18 feet long." An abundance of salmon, shad, and bass—"one of the best fish in the country," taken "sometimes two or three thousand at a set," "some four foot long," left on the sand behind the seine; sometimes used for manure. "Alewives . . . in the latter end of April come up to the fresh rivers to spawn, in such multitudes as is almost incredible, pressing up in such shallow waters as will scarce permit them to swim, having likewise such longing desire after the fresh water ponds, that no beatings with poles, or forcive agitations by other devices, will cause them to return to the sea, till they have cast their spawn."

"The Oysters be great ones in form of a shoe-horn, some be a foot long; these breed on certain banks that are bare every spring tide. This fish without the shell is so big, that it must admit of a division before you can well get it into your mouth." For lobsters, "their plenty makes them little esteemed and seldom eaten." Speaks of "a great oyster bank" in the middle of Back Bay, just off the true mouth of the Charles, and of another in the Mistick. These obstructed the navigation of both rivers.

Journal
January 24, 1855

[*"The grim-fac'd Ounce" is the lynx. "Heath cocks all gone" sums up their status succinctly: the heath hen is extinct. The communal birds that blocked the sun with their nests were passenger pigeons: the passenger pigeon is extinct. The swan was probably the whistling swan—still alive, and with its 85" wingspan, still aloft. The bass is the striped bass.*]

I CANNOT BUT SEE STILL in my mind's eye those little striped breams poised in Walden's glaucous water. They balance all the rest of the world in my estimation at present, for this is the bream that I have just found, and for the time I neglect all its brethren and am ready to kill the fatted calf on its account. For more than two centuries have men fished here and have not distinguished this permanent settler of the township. It is not like a new bird, a transient visitor that may not be seen again for years, but there it dwells and has dwelt permanently, who can tell how long? When my eyes first rested on Walden the striped bream was poised in it, though I did not see it, and when Tahatawan paddled his canoe there. How wild it makes the pond and the township to find a new fish in it! America renews her youth here. But in my account of this bream I cannot go a hair's breadth beyond the mere statement that it exists—the miracle of its existence, my contemporary and neighbor, yet so different from me! I can only poise my thought there by its side and try to think like a bream for a moment. I can only think of precious jewels, of music, poetry, beauty, and the mystery of life. I only see the bream in its orbit, as I see a star, but I care not to measure its distance or weight. The bream, appreciated, floats in the pond as the centre of the system, another image of God. Its life no man can explain more than he can his own. I want you to perceive the mystery of the bream. I have a contemporary in Walden. It has fins where I have legs and arms. I have a friend among the fishes, at least a new acquaintance. Its character will interest me, I trust, not its clothes and anatomy. I do not want it to eat. Acquaintance with it is to make my life more rich and eventful.

Journal
November 30, 1858

AH, THE PICKEREL of Walden! when I see them lying on the ice, or in the well which the fisherman cuts in the ice, making a little hole to admit the water, I am always surprised by their rare beauty, as if they were fabulous fishes, they are so foreign to the streets, even to the woods, foreign as Arabia to our Concord life. They possess a quite dazzling and transcendent beauty which separates them by a wide interval from the cadaverous cod and haddock whose fame is trumpeted in our streets. They are not green like the pines, nor gray like the stones, nor blue like the sky; but they have, to my eyes, if possible, yet rarer colors, like flowers and precious stones, as if they were the pearls, the animalized *nuclei* or crystals of the Walden water. They, of course, are Walden all over and all through; are themselves small Waldens in the animal kingdom, Waldenses. It is surprising that they are caught here— that in this deep and capacious spring, far beneath the rattling teams and chaises and tinkling sleighs that travel the Walden road, this great gold and emerald fish swims. I never chanced to see its kind in any market; it would be the cynosure of all eyes there.

Walden, "The Pond in Winter"

SEE THAT LONG MEANDERING track where a deer mouse hopped over the soft snow last night, scarcely making any impression. What if you could witness with owls' eyes the revelry of the wood mice some night, frisking about the wood like so many little kangaroos? Here is a palpable evidence that the woods are nightly thronged with little creatures which most have never seen—such populousness as commonly only the imagination dreams of.

Journal
January 4, 1860

IT IS REMARKABLE how many creatures live wild and free though secret in the woods, and still sustain themselves in the neighborhood of towns, suspected by hunters only. How retired the otter manages to live here! He grows to be four feet long, as big as a small boy, perhaps without any human being getting a glimpse of him. I formerly saw the raccoon in the woods behind where my house is built, and probably still heard their whinnering at night.

Walden, "Brute Neighbors"

WHAT IS A COUNTRY WITHOUT rabbits and partridges? They are among the most simple and indigenous animal products; ancient and venerable families known to antiquity as to modern times; of the very hue and substance of Nature, nearest allied to leaves and to the ground—and to one another; it is either winged or it is legged. It is hardly as if you had seen a wild creature when a rabbit or a partridge bursts away, only a natural one, as much to be expected as rustling leaves. The partridge and the rabbit are still sure to thrive, like true natives of the soil, whatever revolutions occur. If the forest is cut off, the sprouts and bushes which spring up afford them concealment, and they become more numerous than ever. That must be a poor country indeed that does not support a hare. Our woods teem with them both, and around every swamp may be seen the partridge or rabbit walk, beset with twiggy fences and horse-hair snares, which some cow-boy tends.

Walden, "Winter Animals"

I THINK THAT THE MOST important requisite in describing an animal, is to be sure and give its character and spirit, for in that you have, without error, the sum and effect of all its parts, known and unknown. You must tell what it is to man. Surely the most important part of an animal is its *anima*, its vital spirit, on which is based its character and all the peculiarities by which it most concerns us. Yet most scientific books which treat of animals leave this out altogether, and what they describe are as it were phenomena of dead matter.

Journal
February 18, 1860

Going along the steep side-hill on the south of the pond about 4 p.m., on the edge of the little patch of wood which the choppers have not yet levelled—though they have felled many an acre around it this winter—I observed a rotten and hollow hemlock stump about two feet high and six inches in diameter, and instinctively approached with my right hand ready to cover it. I found a flying squirrel in it, which, as my left hand had covered a small hole at the bottom, ran directly into my right hand.

Journal
March 22, 1855

I was amused with the behavior of two red squirrels as I approached the hemlocks. They were as gray as red, and white beneath. I at first heard a faint, sharp chirp, like a bird, within the hemlock, on my account, and then one rushed forward on a descending limb toward me, barking or chirruping at me after his fashion, within a rod. They seemed to vie with one another who should be most bold. For four or five minutes at least, they kept up an incessant chirruping or squeaking bark, vibrating their tails and their whole bodies and frequently changing their position or point of view, making a show of rushing forward, or perhaps darting off a few feet like lightning and barking still more loudly, *i.e.* with a yet sharper exclamation, as if frightened by their own motions; their whole bodies quivering, their heads and great eyes on the *qui vive*. You are uncertain whether it is not half in sport after all.

Journal
March 11, 1860

I see a woodchuck on the side of Lupine Hill, eight or ten rods off. He runs to within three feet of his hole; then stops, with his head up. His whole body makes an angle of forty-five degrees as I look sideways at it. I see his shining black eyes and black snout and his little erect ears. He is of a light brown forward at this distance (hoary above, yellowish or sorrel beneath), gradually darkening backward to the end of the tail, which is dark-brown. The general aspect is grizzly, the ends of most of the hairs being white. The yellowish brown, or rather sorrel, of his

94

throat and breast very like the sand of his burrow, over which it is slanted. No glaring distinctions to catch the eye and betray him.

Journal
April 29, 1855

HAVING STOOD QUITE STILL on the edge of the ditch close to the north edge of the maple swamp some time, and heard a slight rustling near me from time to time, I looked round and saw a mink under the bushes within a few feet. It was pure reddish-brown above, with a blackish and somewhat bushy tail, a blunt nose, and somewhat innocent-looking head. It crept along toward me and around me, *within two feet*, in a semicircle, snuffing the air, and pausing to look at me several times.

Journal
April 15, 1858

SEE A BROAD AND DISTINCT otter-trail, made last night or yester-day. It came out to the river through the low woods north of Pinxter Swamp, making a very conspicuous trail, from seven to nine or ten inches wide and three or four deep, with sometimes singularly upright sides, as if a square timber had been drawn along, but commonly rounded. It made some short turns and zigzags; passed *under* limbs which were only five inches above the snow, not over them; had apparently slid down all banks and declivities, making a uniform broad hollow trail there without any mark of its feet.

Journal
February 20, 1856

As I STOOD BY THE LAST hole, I heard the old fox bark, and saw her near the brow of the hill on the northwest, amid the bushes, restless and anxious, overlooking me a dozen or fourteen rods off. I was, no doubt, by the hole in which the young were. She uttered at very short intervals a prolonged, shrill, screeching kind of bark, beginning lower and rising to a very high key, lasting two seconds; a very broken and ragged sound, more like the scream of a large and angry bird than the bark of a dog, trilled like a piece of vibrating metal at the end. It moved restlessly back and forth, or approached nearer, and stood or sat on its haunches like a dog with its tail laid out in a curve on one side, and when it barked it laid its ears flat back and stretched its nose forward.

Journal
May 20, 1858

WE WERE NOT SO LUCKY as to hear wolves howl, though that is an occasional serenade. Some friends of mine, who two years ago went up the Caucomgomoc River, were serenaded by wolves while moose-hunting by moonlight. It was a sudden burst, as if a hundred demons had broke loose—a startling sound enough, which, if any, would make your hair stand on end, and all was still again. It lasted but a moment, and you'd have thought there were twenty of them, when probably there were only two or three. They heard it twice only, and they said that it gave expression to the wilderness which it lacked before.

The Maine Woods, "Allegash"

GEORGE MELVIN CAME TO TELL ME this forenoon that a strange animal was killed on Sunday, the 9th, near the north line of the town, and it was not known certainly what it was. From his description I judged it to be a Canada lynx. In the afternoon I went to see it. It was killed on Sunday morning by John Quincy Adams, who lives in Carlisle about half a mile (or less) from the Concord line, on the Carlisle road. . . . I measured the stuffed skin carefully.

Journal
September 11, 1860

THE MOST INTERESTING SIGHT I saw in Brattleboro was the skin and skull of a panther (Felis concolor) (cougar, catamount, painter, American lion, puma), which was killed, according to a written notice attached, on the 15th of June by the Saranac Club of Brattleboro, six young men, on a fishing and hunting excursion. This paper described it as eight feet in extreme length and weighing one hundred and ten pounds. The Brattleboro newspaper says its body was "4 feet 11 inches in length, and the tail 2 feet 9 inches; the animal weighed 108 pounds." I was

surprised at its great size and apparent strength. It gave one a
new idea of our American forests and the vigor of nature here.
It was evident that it could level a platoon of men with a stroke
of its paw. I was particularly impressed by the size of its limbs,
the size of its canine teeth, and its great white claws. I do not
see but this affords a sufficient foundation for the stories of the
lion heard and its skins seen near Boston by the first settlers.

Journal
September 9, 1856

Whereupon he began to push the canoe back rapidly, and we
had receded thus half a dozen rods, when we suddenly spied
two moose standing just on the edge of the open part of the
meadow which we had passed, not more than six or seven rods
distant, looking round the alders at us. They made me think of
great frightened rabbits, with their long ears and half inquisi-
tive half frightened looks; the true denizens of the forest.

The Maine Woods,
"Chesuncook"

The globe is the richer for the variety of its inhabitants.

Journal
May 17, 1854

"The magical
moon with
attendant stars"

MOONLIGHT ON FAIR HAVEN POND seen from the Cliffs. A sheeny lake in the midst of a boundless forest, the windy surf sounding freshly and wildly in the single pine behind you; the silence of hushed wolves in the wilderness, and, as you fancy, moose looking off from the shore of the lake. The stars of poetry and history and unexplored nature looking down on the scene. This is my world now, with a dull whitish mark curving northward through the forest marking the outlet to the lake. Fair Haven by moonlight lies there like a lake in the Maine wilderness in the midst of a primitive forest untrodden by man. This light and this hour take the civilization all out of the landscape.

Journal
September 5, 1851

IF THERE IS A MORE SPLENDID moonlight than usual, only the belated traveller observes it. When I am outside, on the outskirts of the town, enjoying the still majesty of the moon, I am wont to think that all men are aware of this miracle, that they too are silently worshipping this manifestation of divinity elsewhere. But when I go into the house I am undeceived; they are absorbed in checkers or chess or novel, though they may have been advertised of the brightness through the shutters. In the moonlight night what intervals are created!

Journal
May 16, 1851

By MOONLIGHT ALL IS SIMPLE. We are enabled to erect ourselves, our minds, on account of the fewness of objects. We are no longer distracted. It is simple as bread and water. It is simple as the rudiments of an art—a lesson to be taken before sunlight, perchance, to prepare us for that.

Journal
September 22, 1854

AND I FORGOT TO SAY that after I reached the road by Potter's bars—or further, by Potter's Brook—I saw the moon suddenly reflected full from a pool. A puddle from which you may see the moon reflected, and the earth dissolved under your feet. The magical moon with attendant stars suddenly looking up with mild lustre from a window in the dark earth.

Journal
June 13, 1851

THE GREAT STORY of the night is the moon's adventures with the clouds. What innumerable encounters she has had with them.

Journal
June 25, 1852

NOT MUCH BEFORE 10 o'CLOCK does the moonlight night begin. When man is asleep and day fairly forgotten, then is the beauty of moonlight seen over lonely pastures where cattle are silently feeding. Then let me walk in a diversified country, of hill and dale, with heavy woods one side, and copses and scattered trees and bushes enough to give me shadows.

Journal
June 14, 1851

IT ADDS A CHARM, a dignity, a glory, to the earth to see the light of the moon reflected from her streams.

Journal
August 12, 1851

MOONLIGHT IS THE BEST restorer of antiquity. The houses in the village have a classical elegance as of the best days of Greece, and this half-finished church reminds me of the Parthenon, or whatever is most famous and excellent in art. So serene it stands, reflecting the moon, and intercepting the stars with its rafters, as if it were refreshed by the dews of the night equally with me. By day Mr. Hosmer, but by night Vitruvius rather. If it were always to stand in this mild and sombre light it would be finished already. It is in progress by day but completed by night, and already its designer is an old master.

Journal
September 3, 1841

Is NOT THE MIDNIGHT like Central Africa to most of us? Are we not tempted to explore it—to penetrate to the shores of its lake Tchad, and discover the source of its Nile, perchance the Mountains of the Moon? Who knows what fertility and beauty, moral and natural, are there to be found? In the Mountains of the Moon, in the Central Africa of the night, there is where all Niles have their hidden heads.

"Night and Moonlight"

THE STARS ARE THE JEWELS of the night, and perchance surpass anything which day has to show. A companion with whom I was sailing one very windy but bright moonlight night, when the stars were few and faint, thought that a man could get along with *them*—though he was considerably reduced in his circumstances—that they were a kind of bread and cheese that never failed.

"Night and Moonlight"

The stars are the apexes of what wonderful triangles! What distant and different beings in the various mansions of the universe are contemplating the same one at the same moment!

Walden, "Economy"

When I consider how, after sunset, the stars come out gradually in troops from behind the hills and woods, I confess that I could not have contrived a more curious and inspiring night.

Journal
July 26, 1840

"The beauty of the sunset or the rainbow"

THERE ARE METEOROLOGISTS, but who keeps a record of the fairer sunsets? While men are recording the direction of the wind, they neglect to record the beauty of the sunset or the rainbow. The sun not yet set.

Journal
June 28, 1852

IF I WERE TO CHOOSE A TIME for a friend to make a passing visit to this world for the first time, in the full possession of all his faculties, perchance it would be at a moment when the sun was setting with splendor in the west, his light reflected far and wide through the clarified air after a rain, and a brilliant rainbow, as now, o'erarching the eastern sky.

Journal
August 7, 1852

WE NEVER TIRE of the drama of sunset. I go forth each afternoon and look into the west a quarter of an hour before sunset, with fresh curiosity, to see what new picture will be painted there, what new panorama exhibited, what new dissolving views. Can Washington Street or Broadway show anything as good? Every day a new picture is painted and framed, held up for half an hour, in such lights as the Great Artist chooses, and then withdrawn, and the curtain falls.

> Journal
> January 7, 1852

THE MAN IS BLESSED WHO every day is permitted to behold anything so pure and serene as the western sky at sunset, while revolutions vex the world.

> Journal
> December 27, 1851

THERE WAS A REMARKABLE sunset; a mother-of-pearl sky seen over the Price farm; some small clouds, as well as the edges of large ones, most brilliantly painted with mother-of-pearl tints through and through. I never saw the like before. Who can foretell the sunset—what it will be?

> Journal
> January 10, 1851

THE GRANDEST PICTURE in the world is the sunset sky.

> Journal
> July 26, 1852

WE HAD A REMARKABLE SUNSET one day last November. I was walking in a meadow, the source of a small brook, when the sun at last, just before setting, after a cold gray day, reached a clear stratum in the horizon, and the softest, brightest morning sunlight fell on the dry grass and on the stems of the trees in the opposite horizon and on the leaves of the shrub-oaks on the hillside, while our shadows stretched long over the meadow eastward, as if we were the only motes in its beams. It was such a light as we could not have imagined a moment before, and the air also was so warm and serene that nothing was wanting to make a paradise of that meadow. When we reflected that this was not a solitary phenomenon, never to happen again, but that it would happen forever and ever an infinite number of evenings, and cheer and reassure the latest child that walked there, it was more glorious still.

"Walking"

IF MEN WERE TO BE destroyed and the books they have written were to be transmitted to a new race of creatures, in a new world, what kind of record would be found in them of so remarkable a phenomenon as the rainbow?

Journal
March 13, 1859

THE RAINBOW, AFTER ALL, does not attract an attention proportionate to its singularity and beauty. Moses was the last to comment on it. It is a phenomenon more aside from the common course of nature. Too distinctly a sign or symbol of something to be disregarded. What form of beauty could be imagined more striking and conspicuous? An arch of the most brilliant and glorious colors completely spanning the heavens before the eyes of men! Children look at it. It is wonderful that all men do not take pains to behold it. At some waterfalls it is permanent, as long as the sun shines.

Journal
August 6, 1852

IS NOT THE RAINBOW a faint vision of God's face? How glorious should be the life of man passed under this arch! What more remarkable phenomenon than a rainbow, yet how little it is remarked!

Journal
June 22, 1852

I SAW HERE THE MOST BRILLIANT rainbow that I ever imagined. It was just across the stream below the precipice, formed on the mist which this tremendous fall produced; and I stood on a level with the key-stone of its arch. It was not a few faint prismatic colors merely, but a full semicircle, only four or five rods in diameter, though as wide as usual, so intensely bright as to pain the eye.

"A Yankee in Canada"
(The Walls of Quebec)

About 3 p.m. I noticed a distinct fragment of rainbow, about as long as wide, on each side of the sun, one north and the other south and at the same height above the horizon with the sun, all in a line parallel with the horizon; and, as I thought, there was a slight appearance of a bow.

The sun-dogs, if that is their name, were not so distinctly bright as an ordinary rainbow, but were plainly orange-yellow and a peculiar light violet-blue, the last color looking like a hole in the cloud, or a thinness through which you saw the sky.

Journal
February 2, 1860

[These dry weather rainbows are known as sun dogs, though meteorologists prefer to call them parhelions or solar arcs. In the continental United States, a well-defined sun dog arches from horizon over the sun and back down to horizon. The sides of the half-circle near the horizon have rainbow colors brighter than the rest of the arc, which is often faint or invisible.

The sun dog, created by the bending of sunlight through certain types of ice crystals, is a cold weather phenomenon. The sun dogs I have seen— all in the South, in North Carolina and Georgia—occurred on sunny or slightly overcast days with high, thin clouds.]

We see the rainbow apparently when we are on the edge of the rain, just as the sun is setting. If we are too deep in the rain, then it will appear dim. Sometimes it is so near that I see a portion of its arch this side of the woods in the horizon, tinging them. Sometimes we are completely within it, enveloped by it, and experience the realization of the child's wish. The obvious colors are red and green. Why green? It is astonishing how brilliant the red may be. What is the difference between that red and the ordinary red of the evening sky? Who does not feel that here is a phenomenon which natural philosophy alone is inadequate to explain? The use of the rainbow, who has described it?

Journal
August 7, 1852

ONCE IT CHANCED THAT I stood in the very abutment of a rainbow's arch, which filled the lower stratum of the atmosphere, tinging the grass and leaves around, and dazzling me as if I looked through colored crystal. It was a lake of rainbow light, in which, for a short while, I lived like a dolphin. If it had lasted longer it might have tinged my employments and life.

Walden, "Baker Farm"

"Our maker, our abode, our destiny"

HEAVEN IS UNDER our feet as well as over our heads.

Walden, "The Pond in Winter"

WHEN THE COMMON MAN looks into the sky, which he has not so much profaned, he thinks it less gross than the earth, and with reverence speaks of "the Heavens," but the seer will in the same sense speak of "the Earths," and his Father who is in them.

A *Week*, "Friday"

HOW LITTLE APPRECIATION of the beauty of the landscape there is among us! We have to be told that the Greeks called the world Beauty, or Order, but we do not see clearly why they did so, and we esteem it at best only a curious philological fact.

"Walking"

THE EARTH IS NOT A MERE fragment of dead history, stratum upon stratum like the leaves of a book, to be studied by geologists and antiquaries chiefly, but living poetry like the leaves of a tree, which precede flowers and fruit—not a fossil earth, but a living earth; compared with whose great central life all animal and vegetable life is merely parasitic.

Walden, "Spring"

I SEE THAT ALL IS NOT GARDEN and cultivated field and crops, that there are square rods in Middlesex County as purely primitive and wild as they were a thousand years ago, which have escaped the plow and the axe and the scythe and the cranberry-rake, little oases of wildness in the desert of our civilization, wild as a square rod on the moon, supposing it to be uninhabited. I believe almost in the personality of such planetary matter, feel something akin to reverence for it, can even worship it as terrene, titanic matter extant in my day. . . . These spots are meteoric, aerolitic, and such matter has in all ages been worshipped. Aye, when we are lifted out of the slime and film of our habitual life, we see the whole globe to be an aerolite, and reverence it as such, and make pilgrimages to it, far off as it is. How happens it that we reverence the stones which fall from another planet, and not the stones which belong to this—another globe, not this—heaven, and not earth? Are not the stones in Hodge's wall as good as the aerolite at Mecca? Is not our broad back-door-stone as good as any corner-stone in heaven?

Journal
August 30, 1856

ON THE OUTSIDE all the life of the earth is expressed in the animal or vegetable, but make a deep cut in it and you find it vital; you find in the very sands an anticipation of the vegetable leaf. No wonder, then, that plants grow and spring in it. The atoms have already learned the law. Let a vegetable sap convey it upwards and you have a vegetable leaf. No wonder that the earth expresses itself outwardly in leaves, which labors with the idea thus inwardly. The overhanging leaf sees here its prototype. The earth is pregnant with law.

Journal
March 2, 1854

You must love the crust of the earth on which you dwell more than the sweet crust of any bread or cake. You must be able to extract nutriment out of a sand-heap. You must have so good an appetite as this, else you will live in vain.

Journal
January 25, 1858

Nature, the earth herself, is the only panacea.

Journal
September 24, 1859

I love nature, I love the landscape, because it is so sincere. It never cheats me. It never jests. It is cheerfully, musically earnest. I lie and relie on the earth.

Journal
November 16, 1850

Where my path crosses the brook in the meadow there is a singularly sweet scent in the heavy air bathing the brakes, where the brakes grow—the fragrance of the earth, as if the dew were a distillation of the fragrant essences of nature.

Journal
June 14, 1851

I see, smell, taste, hear, feel, that everlasting Something to which we are allied, at once our maker, our abode, our destiny, our very Selves; the one historic truth, the most remarkable fact which can become the distinct and uninvited subject of our thought, the actual glory of the universe; the only fact which a human being cannot avoid recognizing, or in some way forget or dispense with.

A Week, "Monday"

COMPARATIVELY, OUR GARDENING is on a petty scale, the gardener still nursing a few asters amid dead weeds, ignorant of the gigantic asters and roses which, as it were, overshadow him and ask for none of his care. Comparatively, it is like a little red paint ground on a teacup and held up against the sunset sky. Why not take more elevated and broader views, walk in the greater garden, not skulk in a little "debauched" nook of it? Consider the beauty of the earth, and not merely of a few impounded herbs? However, you will not see these splendors, whether you stand on the hilltop or in the hollow, unless you are prepared to see them. . . . The beauty of the earth answers exactly to your demand and appreciation.

Journal
November 2, 1858

DEAR TO ME TO LIE IN, this sand; fit to preserve the bones of a race for thousands of years to come. And this is my home, my native soil; and I am a New-Englander. Of thee, O earth, are my bone and sinew made; to thee, O sun, am I brother. . . . To this dust my body will gladly return as to its origin. Here have I my habitat. I am of thee.

Journal
November 7, 1851

AH! IF I COULD SO LIVE that there should be no desultory moment in all my life! that in the trivial season, when small fruits are ripe, my fruits might be ripe also! that I could match nature always with my moods! that in each season when some part of nature especially flourishes, then a corresponding part of me may not fail to flourish! Ah, I would walk, I would sit and sleep, with natural piety! What if I could pray aloud or to myself as I went along by the brooksides a cheerful prayer like the birds! For joy I could embrace the earth; I shall delight to be buried in it.

Journal
August 17, 1851

"Matter appropriated by spirit"

THE SIMPLEST AND MOST LUMPISH fungus has a peculiar interest to us, compared with a mere mass of earth, because it is so obviously organic and related to ourselves, however mute. It is the expression of an idea; growth according to a law; matter not dormant, not raw, but inspired, appropriated by spirit. If I take up a handful of earth, however separately interesting the particles may be, their relation to one another appears to be that of mere juxtaposition generally. I might have thrown them together thus. But the humblest fungus betrays a life akin to my own. It is a successful poem in its kind. There is suggested something superior to any particle of matter, in the idea or mind which uses and arranges the particles.

Journal
October 10, 1858

WE GO ADMIRING THE PURE and delicate tints of fungi on the surface of the damp swamp there, following up along the north side of the brook past the right of the old camp. There are many very beautiful lemon-yellow ones of various forms, some shaped like buttons, some becoming finely scalloped on the edge, some club-shaped and hollow, of the most delicate and rare but decided tints, contrasting well with the decaying leaves about them. There are others also pure white, others a wholesome red, others brown, and some even a light indigo-blue above and beneath and throughout. When colors come to be taught in the schools, as they should be, both the prism (or the rainbow) and these fungi should be used by way of illustration, and if the pupil does not learn colors, he may learn fungi, which perhaps is better. You almost envy the wood frogs and toads that hop amid such gems.

Journal
September 1, 1856

I DID NOT REGRET my not having seen this before, since I now saw it under circumstances so favorable. I was in just the frame of mind to see something wonderful, and this was a phenomenon adequate to my circumstances and expectation, and it put me on the alert to see more like it. I exulted like "a pagan suckled in a creed" that had never been worn at all, but was bran new, and adequate to the occasion. I let science slide, and rejoiced in that light as if it had been a fellow-creature. I saw that it was excellent, and was very glad to know that it was so cheap. A scientific *explanation*, as it is called, would have been altogether out of place there. That is for pale daylight. Science with its retorts would have put me to sleep; it was the opportunity to be ignorant that I improved. It suggested to me that there was something to be seen if one had eyes. It made a believer of me more than before. I believed that the woods were not tenantless, but choke-full of honest spirits as good as myself any day—not an empty chamber, in which chemistry was left to work alone, but an inhabited house—and for a few moments I enjoyed fellowship with them. . . . Long enough I had heard of irrelevant things; now at length I was glad to make acquaintance with the light that dwells in rotten wood.

The Maine Woods, "Allegash"

["The light that dwells in rotten wood," foxfire, is a rare reward for campers, backpackers and those who walk at night. Dayhikers never see it. Foxfire is phosphorescent fungi that glow light green from moist, rotting logs. Beyond that explanation, I too will let science slide.

Every time I have been fortunate enough to witness this startling luminescence in the night-black forest, it has been in a damp, shady spot near a creek or river. On several occasions I have come across a 3- or 4-foot length of foxfire, bright enough to read by with help from the moon. At least that's how I remember them.]

THE GENTIAN, NOW GENERALLY in prime, loves moist, shady banks, and its transcendent blue shows best in the shade and suggests coolness; contrasts there with the fresh green—a splendid blue, light in the shade, turning to purple with age. They are particularly abundant under the north side of the willow-row in Merrick's pasture. I count fifteen in a single cluster there, and afterward twenty at Gentian Lane near Flint's Bridge, and there were other clusters below. Bluer than the bluest sky, they lurk in the moist and shady recesses of the banks.

Journal
September 28, 1856

AT THE BATHING-PLACE there is a hummock which was floated on to the meadow some springs ago, now densely covered with the handsome red-stemmed wild rose, a full but irregular clump, from the ground, showing no bare stems below, but a dense mass of shining leaves and small red stems above in their midst, and on every side now, in the twilight, more than usually beautiful they appear. Countless roses, partly closed, of a very deep rich color, as if the rays of the departed sun still shone through them; a more spiritual rose at this hour, beautifully blushing; and then the unspeakable beauty and promise of those fair swollen buds that spot the mass, which will blossom tomorrow, and the more distant promise of the handsomely formed green ones, which yet show no red, for few things are handsomer than a rosebud in any stage; these mingled with a few pure white elder blossoms and some rosaceous or pinkish meadow-sweet heads. I am confident that there can be nothing so beautiful in any cultivated garden, with all their varieties, as this wild clump.

Journal
July 2, 1852

To my senses the dicksonia fern has the most wild and primitive fragrance, quite unalloyed and untamable, such as no human institutions give out—the early morning fragrance of the world, antediluvian, strength and hope imparting. They who scent it can never faint.

Journal
September 24, 1859

We hug the earth—how rarely we mount! Methinks we might elevate ourselves a little more. We might climb a tree, at least. I found my account in climbing a tree once. It was a tall white pine, on the top of a hill; and though I got well pitched, I was well paid for it, for I discovered new mountains in the horizon which I had never seen before—so much more of the earth and heavens. I might have walked about the foot of the tree for threescore years and ten, and yet I certainly should never have seen them. But, above all, I discovered around me—it was near the end of June—on the ends of the topmost branches only, a few minute and delicate red cone-like blossoms, the fertile flower of the white pine looking heavenward. I carried straightway to the village the topmost spire, and showed it to stranger jurymen who walked the streets—for it was court-week—and to farmers and lumber-dealers and wood-choppers and hunters, and not one had ever seen the like before, but they wondered as at a star dropped down. Tell of ancient architects finishing their works on the tops of columns as perfectly as on the lower and more visible parts! Nature has from the first expanded the minute blossoms of the forest only toward the heavens, above men's heads and unobserved by them. We see only the flowers that are under our feet in the meadows. The pines have developed their delicate blossoms on the highest twigs of the wood every summer for ages, as well over the heads of Nature's red children as of her white ones; yet scarcely a farmer or hunter in the land has ever seen them.

"Walking"

"The beauty
of the
trees"

No ANNUAL TRAINING or muster of soldiery, no celebration with its scarfs and banners, could import into the town a hundredth part of the annual splendor of our October. . . . Let us have a good many maples and hickories and scarlet oaks, then, I say. Blaze away! . . . . Let us have willows for spring, elms for summer, maples and walnuts and tupelos for autumn, evergreens for winter, and oaks for all seasons. What is a gallery in a house to a gallery in the streets! I think that there is not a picture-gallery in the country which would be worth so much to us as is the western view under the elms of our main street.

Journal
October 18, 1858

How THEY ARE MIXED UP, of all species, Oak and Maple and Chestnut and Birch! But Nature is not cluttered with them; she is a perfect husbandman; she stores them all. Consider what a vast crop is thus annually shed on the earth! This, more than any mere grain or seed, is the great harvest of the year. The trees are now repaying the earth with interest what they have taken from it. They are discounting. They are about to add a leaf's thickness to the depth of the soil. This is the beautiful way in which Nature gets her muck, while I chaffer with this man and that, who talks to me about sulphur and the cost of carting. We are all the richer for their decay. I am more interested in this crop than in the English grass alone or in the corn. It prepares the virgin mould for future cornfields and forests, on which the earth fattens. It keeps our homestead in good heart.

For beautiful variety no crop can be compared with this. Here is not merely the plain yellow of the grains, but nearly all the colors that we know, the brightest blue not excepted: the early blushing Maple, the Poison-Sumach blazing its sins as scarlet, the mulberry Ash, the rich chrome yellow of the Poplars, the brilliant red Huckleberry, with which the hills' backs are painted, like those of sheep.

"Autumnal Tints"

LITTLE DID THE FATHERS of the town anticipate this brilliant success, when they caused to be imported from farther in the country some straight poles with their tops cut off, which they called sugar-maples; and, as I remember, after they were set out, a neighboring merchant's clerk, by way of jest, planted beans about them. Those which were then jestingly called bean-poles are today far the most beautiful objects noticeable in our streets. They are worth all and more than they have cost . . . if only because they have filled the open eyes of children with their rich color unstintedly so many Octobers. We will not ask them to yield us sugar in the spring, while they afford us so fair a prospect in the autumn.

"Autumnal Tints"

OUR HUMBLE VILLAGES in the plain are their contribution. We borrow from the forest the boards which shelter and the sticks which warm us. How important is their evergreen to the winter, that portion of the summer which does not fade, the permanent year, the unwithered grass. Thus simply, and with little expense of altitude, is the surface of the earth diversified. What would human life be without forests, those natural cities? From the tops of mountains they appear like smooth-shaven lawns, yet whither shall we walk but in this taller grass?

"A Winter Walk"

SOMETIMES I RAMBLED to pine groves, standing like temples, or like fleets at sea, full-rigged, with wavy boughs, and rippling with light, so soft and green and shady that the Druids would have forsaken their oaks to worship in them; or to the cedar wood beyond Flint's Pond, where the trees, covered with hoary blue berries, spiring higher and higher, are fit to stand before Valhalla, and the creeping juniper covers the ground with wreaths full of fruit; or to swamps where the usnea lichen hangs in festoons from the white-spruce trees, and toadstools.

Walden, "Baker Farm"

F. ANDREW MICHAUX SAYS that "the species of large trees are much more numerous in North America than in Europe: in the United States there are more than one hundred and forty species that exceed thirty feet in height; in France there are but thirty that attain this size, of which eighteen enter into the composition of the forests, and seven only are employed in building."

Journal
January, 1851

[*Francois Michaux was correct about the diversity of our American forests. Since his explorations in the very early 1800s, foresters and botanists have discovered many more species that exceed 30 feet in height. The richness of the Southern Appalachian forest, for instance, is unequaled over most of the world's temperate zone. The most diverse area within the Southern Appalachians—the Great Smoky Mountains National Park, a preserve of only slightly more than 500,000 acres—is home to more native tree species (101) than all of Northern Europe.*]

WE HAVE BUT A FAINT conception of a full-grown oak forest stretching uninterrupted for miles, consisting of sturdy trees from one to three and even four feet in diameter, whose interlacing branches form a complete and uninterrupted canopy. Many trunks old and hollow, in which wild beasts den. Hawks nesting in the dense tops, and deer glancing between the trunks, and occasionally the Indian with a face the color of the faded oak leaf.

Journal
November 10, 1860

TAKE THE MOST RIGID TREE, the whole effect is peculiarly soft and spirit-like, for there is no marked edge or outline. How could you draw the outline of these snowy fingers seen against the fog, without exaggeration? There is no more a boundary-line or circumference that can be drawn, than a diameter. Hardly could the New England farmer drive to market under these trees without feeling that his sense of beauty was addressed. He would be aware that the phenomenon called beauty was become visible, if one were at leisure or had had the right culture to appreciate it. A miller with whom I rode actually remarked on the beauty of the trees; and a farmer told me in all sincerity that, having occasion to go into Walden Woods in his sleigh, he thought he never saw anything so beautiful in all his life, and if there had been men there who knew how to write about it, it would have been a great occasion for them.

Journal
January 18, 1859

AS YOU APPROACH THE WOOD, and even walk through it, the trees do not affect you as large, but as surely as you go quite up to one you are surprised. . . . Such a wood, at the same time that it suggests antiquity, imparts an unusual dignity to the earth.

Journal
November 2, 1860

SOME SINGLE TREES, wholly bright scarlet, seen against others of their kind still freshly green, or against evergreens, are more memorable than whole groves will be by and by. How beautiful, when a whole tree is like one great scarlet fruit full of ripe

119

juices, every leaf, from lowest limb to topmost spire, all aglow, especially if you look toward the sun! What more remarkable object can there be in the landscape? Visible for miles, too fair to be believed. If such a phenomenon occurred but once, it would be handed down by tradition to posterity, and get into the mythology at last.

"Autumnal Tints"

MANY TIMES I THOUGHT that if the particular tree, commonly an elm, under which I was walking or riding were the only one like it in the country, it would be worth a journey across the continent to see it. Indeed, I have no doubt that such journeys would be undertaken on hearing a true account of it. But, instead of being confined to a single tree, this wonder was as cheap and common as the air itself. Every man's wood-lot was a miracle and surprise to him, and for those who could not go so far there were the trees in the street and the weeds in the yard.

Journal
January 18, 1859

MOST WERE NOT AWARE of the size of the great elm till it was cut down. I surprised some a few days ago by saying that when its trunk should lie prostrate it would be higher than the head of the tallest man in the town, and that two such trunks could not stand in the chamber we were then in, which was fifteen feet across; that there would be ample room for a double bedstead on the trunk, nay, that the very dinner-table we were sitting at, with our whole party of seven, chairs and all, around it, might be set there.

Journal
January 22, 1856

[Once abundant throughout most of the eastern United States, the American elm—a large, graceful tree with a broad, distinctively symmetrical crown—was also once the most recognizable tree over much of its range. This elm, especially those grown in the open, regularly reached trunk diameters of 6 feet or more. The very thickest specimens on record attained *diameters of 11 to 13 feet, roughly 33 to 40 feet in girth, measured at breast height.*

Because of their size, longevity and recognizable form, American elms were often chosen for council or meeting trees by the early settlers and the Indians before them.

The American elm has been devastated by the accidentally introduced Dutch elm disease, a fungal affliction spread by beetles. The first outbreak in our country occurred in 1930. Unlike the chestnut, however, the American elm still reaches maturity and successfully reproduces its kind. The species is now classified as having "occasional" occurrence.]

I BELIEVE THAT THERE IS a harmony between the hemlock and the water which it overhangs not explainable. In the first place, its green is especially grateful to the eye the greater part of the year in any locality, and in the winter, by its verdure overhanging and shading the water, it concentrates in itself the beauty of all fluviatile trees. It loves to stand with its foot close to the water, its roots running over the rocks of the shore, and two or more on opposite sides of a brook make the most beautiful frame to a waterscape, especially in deciduous woods, where the light is sombre and not too glaring. It makes the more complete frame because its branches, particularly in young specimens such as I am thinking of, spring from so near the ground, and it makes so dense a mass of verdure. There are many larger hemlocks covering the steep sidehill forming the bank of the Assabet, where they are successively undermined by the water, and they lean at every angle over the water. Some are almost horizontally directed, and almost every year one falls in and is washed away. The place is known as the "Leaning Hemlocks."

Journal
April 1, 1852

HOW WILD AND REFRESHING to see these old black willows of the river-brink, unchanged from the first, which man has never cut for fuel or for timber! Only the muskrat, tortoises, blackbirds, bitterns, and swallows use them.

Journal
November 9, 1855

WITNESS THE BUDS of the native poplar standing gayly out to the frost on the sides of its bare switches. They express a naked confidence. With cheerful heart one could be a sojourner in the wilderness, if he were sure to find there the catkins of the willow or the alder. When I read of them in the accounts of northern adventurers, by Baffin's Bay or Mackenzie's River, I see how even there, too, I could dwell. They are our little vegetable redeemers. Methinks our virtue will hold out till they come again. They are worthy to have had a greater than Minerva or Ceres for their inventor. Who was the benignant goddess that bestowed them on mankind?

"Natural History"

WHEN CHESTNUTS WERE RIPE I laid up half a bushel for winter. It was very exciting at that season to roam the then boundless chestnut woods of Lincoln—they now sleep their long sleep under the railroad—with a bag on my shoulder, and a stick to open burs with in my hand, for I did not always wait for the frost, amid the rustling of leaves and the loud reproofs of the red-squirrels and the jays, whose half-consumed nuts I some-times stole, for the burs which they had selected were sure to contain sound ones. Occasionally I climbed and shook the trees. They grew also behind my house, and one large tree, which almost overshadowed it, was, when in flower, a bouquet which scented the whole neighborhood, but the squirrels and the jays got most of its fruit; the last coming in flocks early in the morning and picking the nuts out of the burs before they fell. I relinquished these trees to them and visited the more distant woods composed wholly of chestnut.

Walden, "House-Warming"

[*The American chestnut was once one of the largest, most abundant and most valuable (to man and wildlife alike) trees in eastern United States. This species was one of five widespread trees (American elm, sycamore, yellow poplar and white oak are the other four) that regularly attained diameters of 6 or more feet in the Eastern forest. The generally recognized maximum size of the American chestnut is 9 to 11 feet in diameter. There are a few reports of former giants over 13 feet in diameter.*

Judged by today's diminished standards, clean-boled eastern trees with a diameter of seven feet seem implausibly large. That there once were single-boled trees 11 to 13 feet in diameter seems mythological.

The near extinction of the American chestnut remains the greatest botanical catastrophe in the recorded history of North America. The chestnut blight, a fungal disease, was accidentally introduced into New York City from eastern Asia in 1904. Within 45 years the bark-ripping blight had spread throughout the tree's contiguous eastern range, virtually destroying every mature chestnut. For 30 years and more their gray snags were part of the landscape. Today their mossy trunks lie on the forest floor as slowly rotting monuments to America's primeval grandeur.

Fortunately, the American chestnut will avoid extinction. After all these years their stump sprouts, anthropomorphically heroic, continue to reach sapling size before they succumb to the disease and send up another doomed sprout. There are also disjunct populations, both natural and planted, where the blight is not a threat. Scientists have developed hybrid, blight-resistant chestnuts. They won't be as massive as the American chestnut, but they might provide much needed mast for eastern wildlife in the future.]

A CLUMP OF WHITE PINES, seen far westward over the shrub oak plain, which is now lit up by the setting sun, a soft, feathery grove, with their gray stems indistinctly seen, like human beings come to their cabin door, standing expectant on the edge of the plain, impress me with a mild humanity. The trees indeed have hearts. With a certain affection the sun seems to send its farewell ray far and level over the copses to them, and they silently receive it with gratitude, like a group of settlers with their children. The pines impress me as human. A slight vaporous cloud floats high over them, while in the west the sun goes down apace behind glowing pines, and golden clouds like mountains skirt the horizon.

Nothing stands up more free from blame in this world than a pine tree.

Journal
December 20, 1851

THIS AFTERNOON, BEING ON Fair Haven Hill, I heard the sound of a saw, and soon after from the Cliff saw two men sawing down a noble pine beneath, about forty rods off. I resolved to watch it till it fell, the last of a dozen or more which were left when the forest was cut and for fifteen years have waved in solitary majesty over the sprout-land. I saw them like beavers or insects gnawing at the trunk of this noble tree, the diminutive manikins with their cross-cut saw which could scarcely span it. It towered up a hundred feet as I afterward found by measurement, one of the tallest probably in the township and straight as an arrow, but slanting a little toward the hillside, its top seen against the frozen river and the hills of Conantum. I watch closely to see when it begins to move. Now the sawers stop, and with an axe open it a little on the side toward which it leans, that it may break the faster. And now their saw goes again. Now surely it is going; it is inclined one quarter of the quadrant, and, breathless, I expect its crashing fall. But no, I was mistaken; it has not moved an inch; it stands at the same angle as at first. It is fifteen minutes yet to its fall. Still its branches wave in the wind, as if it were destined to stand for a century, and the wind soughs through its needles as of yore; it is still a forest tree, the most majestic tree that waves over Musketaquid. The silvery sheen of the sunlight is reflected from its needles; it still affords an inaccessible crotch for the squirrel's nest; not a lichen has forsaken its mast-like stem, its raking mast—the hill is the hulk. Now, now's the moment! The manikins at its base are fleeing from their crime. They have dropped the guilty saw and axe. How slowly and majestically it starts! as if it were only swayed by a summer breeze, and would return without a sigh to its location in the air. And now it fans the hillside with its fall, and it lies down to its bed in the valley, from which it is never to rise, as softly as a feather, folding its green mantle about it like a warrior, as if, tired of standing, it embraced the earth with silent joy, returning its elements to the dust again. But hark! there you only saw, but did not hear. There now comes up a deafening crash to these rocks, advertising you that even trees do not die without a groan. It rushes to embrace the earth, and mingle its elements with the dust. And now all is still once more and forever, both to eye and ear.

I went down and measured it. It was about four feet in diameter where it was sawed, about one hundred feet long. Before I had reached it the axemen had already half divested it of its branches. Its gracefully spreading top was a perfect wreck on the hillside as if it had been made of glass, and the tender cones of one year's growth upon its summit appealed in vain and too late to the mercy of the chopper. Already he has measured it with his axe, and marked off the mill-logs it will make. And the space it occupied in upper air is vacant for the next two centuries. It is lumber. He has laid waste the air. When the fish hawk in the spring revisits the banks of the Musketaquid, he will circle in vain to find his accustomed perch, and the hen-hawk will mourn for the pines lofty enough to protect her brood. A plant which it has taken two centuries to perfect, rising by slow stages into the heavens, has this afternoon ceased to exist. Its sapling top had expanded to this

January thaw as the forerunner of summers to come. Why does not the village bell sound a knell? I hear no knell tolled. I see no procession of mourners in the streets, or the woodland aisles. The squirrel has leaped to another tree; the hawk has circled further off, and has now settled upon a new eyrie, but the woodman is preparing to lay his axe at the root of that also.

Journal
December 30, 1851

PART 3

"Let Men Tread Gently through Nature"

WHAT IS THE USE OF A HOUSE *if you haven't got a tolerable planet to put it on?*

Letter to Harrison Blake
May 20, 1860

"Sic transit gloria ruris"

EVERY LARGER TREE which I knew and admired is being gradually culled out and carried to mill. I see one or two more large oaks in E. Hubbard's wood lying high on stumps, waiting for snow to be removed. I miss them as surely and with the same feeling that I do the old inhabitants out of the village street. To me they were something more than timber; to their owner not so.

Journal
December 3, 1855

THIS WINTER THEY ARE cutting down our woods more seriously than ever—Fair Haven Hill, Walden, Linnaea Borealis Wood, etc., etc. Thank God they cannot cut down the clouds!

Journal
January 21, 1852

THESE WOODS! WHY DO I not feel their being cut more sorely? Does it not affect me dearly? The axe can deprive me of much.

Concord is sheared of its pride. I am certainly the less attached to my native town in consequence. One, and a main, link is broken. I shall go to Walden less frequently.

Journal
January 24, 1852

When I first paddled a boat on Walden, it was completely surrounded by thick and lofty pine and oak woods, and in some of its coves grape-vines had run over the trees next to the water and formed bowers under which a boat could pass. The hills which form its shores are so steep, and the woods on them were then so high, that, as you looked down from the west end, it had the appearance of an amphitheatre for some kind of sylvan spectacle. I have spent many an hour, when I was younger, floating over its surface as the zephyr willed, having paddled my boat to the middle, and lying on my back across the seats, in a summer forenoon, dreaming awake, until I was aroused by the boat touching the sand, and I arose to see what shore my fates had impelled me to; days when idleness was the most attractive and productive industry. Many a forenoon have I stolen away, preferring to spend thus the most valued part of the day; for I was rich, if not in money, in sunny hours and summer days, and spent them lavishly; nor do I regret that I did not waste more of them in the workshop or the teacher's desk. But since I left those shores the woodchoppers have still further laid them waste, and now for many a year there will be no more rambling through the aisles of the wood, with occasional vistas through which you see the water. My Muse may be excused if she is silent henceforth. How can you expect the birds to sing when their groves are cut down?

Walden, "The Ponds"

I think it would be worth the while to introduce a school of children to such a grove, that they may get an idea of the primitive oaks before they are all gone, instead of hiring botanists to lecture to them when it is too late. Why, you do not now often meet with a respectable oak stump even, for they too have decayed.

Journal
November 2, 1860

I FEAR THAT HE WHO WALKS over these hills a century hence will not know the pleasure of knocking off wild apples. Ah, poor man! there are many pleasures which he will be debarred from!

Journal
November 16, 1850

IT IS OBSERVABLE THAT not only the moose and the wolf disappear before the civilized man, but even many species of insects, such as the black fly and the almost microscopic "no-see-em." How imperfect a notion have we commonly of what was the actual condition of the place where we dwell, three centuries ago!

Journal
January 29, 1856

I SPEND A CONSIDERABLE portion of my time observing the habits of the wild animals, my brute neighbors. By their various movements and migrations they fetch the year about to me. Very significant are the flight of geese and the migration of suckers, etc., etc. But when I consider that the nobler animals have been exterminated here—the cougar, panther, lynx, wolverine, wolf, bear, moose, deer, the beaver, the turkey, etc., etc.—I cannot but feel as if I lived in a tamed, and, as it were, emasculated country. Would not the motions of those larger and wilder animals have been more significant still? Is it not a maimed and imperfect nature that I am conversant with? As if I were to study a tribe of Indians that had lost all its warriors. Do not the forest and the meadow now lack expression, now that I never see nor think of the moose with a lesser forest on his head in the one, nor of the beaver in the other? When I think what were the various sounds and notes, the migrations and works, and changes of fur and plumage which ushered in the spring and marked the other seasons of the year, I am reminded that this my life in nature, this particular round of natural phenomena which I call a year, is lamentably incomplete. I listen to a concert in which so many parts are wanting. The whole civilized country is to some extent turned into a city, and I am that citizen whom I pity. Many of those animal migrations and other phenomena by which the Indians marked the season are no longer to be observed. I seek acquaintance with Nature—to know her moods and manners. Primitive Nature is the most interesting to me. I take infinite pains to know all the phenomena of the spring, for instance, thinking that I have here the entire poem, and then, to my chagrin, I hear that it is but an imperfect copy that I possess and have read, that my ancestors have torn out many of the first leaves and grandest passages, and mutilated it in many places. I should not like to think that some demigod had come before me and picked out some of the best of the stars. I wish to know an entire heaven and an entire earth. All the great trees and beasts, fishes and fowl are gone. The streams, perchance, are somewhat shrunk.

Journal
March 23, 1856

BUT WE FOUND THAT the frontiers were not this way any longer. This generation has come into the world fatally late for some enterprises. Go where we will on the *surface* of things, men have been there before us.

A Week, "Thursday"

IF SALMON, SHAD, and alewives were pressing up our river now, as formerly they were, a good part of the villagers would thus, no doubt, be drawn to the brink at this season. Many inhabitants of the neighborhood of the ponds in Lakeville, Freetown, Fairhaven, etc., have petitioned the legislature for permission to connect Little Quitticus Pond with the Acushnet River by digging, so that the herring can come up into it. The very fishes in countless schools are driven out of a river by the *improvements* of the civilized man, as the pigeon and other fowls out of the air. I can hardly imagine a greater change than this produced by the influence of man in nature. Our Concord River is a dead stream in more senses than we had supposed. In what sense now does the spring ever come to the river, when the sun is not reflected from the scales of a single salmon, shad, or alewife? No doubt there is *some* compensation for this loss, but I do not at this moment see clearly what it is. That river which the aboriginal and indigenous fishes have not deserted is a more primitive and interesting river to me. It is as if some vital quality were to be lost out of a man's blood and it were to circulate more lifelessly through his veins. We are reduced to a few migrating suckers, perchance.

Journal
April 11, 1857

[See the "Sweet wild birds" category for a further description of the passenger pigeon.]

BUT AH WE HAVE FALLEN on evil days! I hear of pickers ordered out of the huckleberry fields, and I see stakes set up with written notices forbidding any to pick them. Some let their fields or allow so much for the picking. Sic transit gloria ruris. I do not mean to blame any, but all—to bewail our fates generally. We are not grateful enough that we have lived a part of our lives before these things occurred. What becomes of the true value of country life—what, if you must go to market for it? It has come to this, that the butcher now brings round our huckleberries in his cart. Why, it is as if the hangman were to perform the marriage ceremony. Such is the inevitable tendency of our civilization, to reduce huckleberries to a level with beef-steaks—that is to blot out four fifths of it, or the going a-huckleberrying, and leave only a pudding, that part which is the fittest accompaniment to a beef-steak. . . .

I suspect that the inhabitants of England and the continent of Europe have thus lost in a measure their natural rights, with the increase of population and monopolies. The wild fruits of the earth disappear before civilization, or only the husks of them are to be found in large markets. The whole country becomes, as it were, a town or beaten common, and almost the only fruits left are a few hips and haws. . . .

What I chiefly regret in this case, is the in effect dog-in-the-manger result; for at the same time that we exclude mankind from gathering berries in our field, we exclude them from gathering health and happiness and inspiration, and a hundred other far finer and nobler fruits than berries, which are found there, but which we have no notion of gathering and shall not gather ourselves, nor ever carry to market, for there is no market for them, but let them rot on the bushes.

We thus strike only one more blow at a simple and wholesome relation to nature.

"Huckleberries"

[Sic transit gloria ruris *literally means "so goes the glory of the countryside" or, idiomatically, "the glory of the countryside passes away."*]

"Ye disgrace earth"

THE ANGLO-AMERICAN CAN indeed cut down, and grub up all this waving forest, and make a stump speech, and vote for Buchanan on its ruins, but he cannot converse with the spirit of the tree he fells, he cannot read the poetry and mythology which retire as he advances. He ignorantly erases mythological tablets in order to print his handbills and town-meeting warrants on them. Before he has learned his a b c in the beautiful but mystic lore of the wilderness which Spenser and Dante had just begun to read, he cuts it down, coins a *pine-tree* shilling (as if to signify the pine's value to him), puts up a *dee*strict school-house, and introduces Webster's spelling-book.

The Maine Woods, "Allegash"

NOWADAYS ALMOST ALL man's improvements, so called, as the building of houses, and the cutting down of the forest and of all large trees, simply deform the landscape, and make it more and more tame and cheap. A people who would begin by burning the fences and let the forest stand! I saw the fences half consumed, their ends lost in the middle of the prairie, and some worldly miser with a surveyor looking after his bounds, while heaven had taken place around him, and he did not see the angels going to and fro, but was looking for an old post-hole in the midst of paradise. I looked again, and saw him standing in the middle of a boggy stygian fen, surrounded by devils, and he had found his bounds without a doubt, three little stones, where a stake had been driven, and looking nearer, I saw that the Prince of Darkness was his surveyor.

"Walking"

To make a railroad round the world available to all mankind is equivalent to grading the whole surface of the planet. Men have an indistinct notion that if they keep up this activity of joint stocks and spades long enough all will at length ride somewhere, in next to no time, and for nothing; but though a crowd rushes to the depot, and the conductor shouts "All aboard!" when the smoke is blown away and the vapor condensed, it will be perceived that a few are riding, but the rest are run over—and it will be called, and will be, "A melancholy accident." No doubt they can ride at last who shall have earned their fare, that is, if they survive so long, but they will probably have lost their elasticity and desire to travel by that time. This spending of the best part of one's life earning money in order to enjoy a questionable liberty during the least valuable part of it, reminds me of the Englishman who went to India to make a fortune first, in order that he might return to England and live the life of a poet. He should have gone up garret at once.

Walden, "Economy"

By avarice and selfishness, and a grovelling habit, from which none of us is free, of regarding the soil as property, or the means of acquiring property chiefly, the landscape is deformed, husbandry is degraded with us.

Walden, "The Bean-Field"

THIS WAS WHAT THOSE SCAMPS did in California. The trees were so grand and venerable that they could not afford to let them grow a hair's breadth bigger, or live a moment longer to reproach themselves. They were so big that they resolved they should never be bigger. They were so venerable that they cut them right down. It was not for the sake of the wood; it was only because they were very grand and venerable.

Journal
October 12, 1857

THE RACE THAT SETTLES and clears the land has got to deal with every tree in the forest in succession. It must be resolute and industrious, and even the stumps must be got out—or are. It is a thorough process, this war with the wilderness—breaking nature, taming the soil, feeding it on oats. The civilized man regards the pine tree as his enemy. He will fell it and let in the light, grub it up and raise wheat or rye there. It is no better than a fungus to him.

Journal
February 2, 1852

[The enemy has changed, but the principle is the same. Today's civilized man often regards the quick-growing pine as his economic friend. Pines are now the row crops whose fields must be cleared and protected. And the native American hardwoods are now hacked and poisoned like tall weeds in the corn.]

THE HEN-HAWK AND THE PINE are friends. The same thing which keeps the hen-hawk in the woods, away from the cities, keeps me here. That bird settles with confidence on a white pine top and not upon your weathercock. That bird will not be poultry of yours, lays no eggs for you, forever hides its nest. Though willed, or *wild*, it is not willful in its wildness. The unsympathizing man regards the wildness of some animals, their strangeness to him, as a sin; as if all their virtue consisted in their tamableness. He has always a charge in his gun ready for their extermination. What we call wildness is a civilization other than our own. The hen-hawk shuns the farmer, but it seeks the friendly shelter and support of the pine. It will not consent to walk in the barn-yard, but it loves to soar above the clouds. It has its own way and is beautiful, when we would fain subject it to our will.

Journal
February 16, 1859

I SEE A BRUTE WITH A GUN in his hand, standing motionless over a musquash-house which he has destroyed. I find that he has visited every one in the neighborhood of Fair Haven Pond, above and below, and broken them all down, laying open the interior to the water, and then stood watchful, close by, for the poor creature to show its head there for a breath of air. There lies the red carcass of one whose pelt he has taken on the spot, flat on the bloody ice. And for his afternoon's cruelty that fellow will be rewarded with a ninepence, perchance. When I consider what are the opportunities of the civilized man for getting ninepences and getting light, this seems to me more savage than savages are. Depend on it that whoever thus treats the musquash's house, his refuge when the water is frozen thick, he and his family will not come to a good end.

Journal
December 26, 1859

THE AFTERNOON'S TRAGEDY, and my share in it, as it affected the innocence, destroyed the pleasure of my adventure. It is true, I came as near as is possible to come to being a hunter and miss it, myself; and as it is, I think that I could spend a year in the woods, fishing and hunting just enough to sustain myself, with satisfaction. This would be next to living like a philosopher on the fruits of the earth which you had raised, which also attracts me. But this hunting of the moose merely for the satisfaction of killing him—not even for the sake of his hide—without making any extraordinary exertion or running any risk yourself, is too much like going out by night to some woodside pasture and shooting your neighbor's horses. These are God's own horses, poor, timid creatures, that will run fast enough as soon as they smell you, though they *are* nine feet high. Joe told us of some hunters who a year or two before had shot down several oxen by night, somewhere in the Maine woods, mistaking them for moose. And so might any of the hunters; and what is the difference in the sport, but the name? In the former case, having killed one of God's and *your own* oxen, you strip off its hide—because that is the common trophy, and, moreover, you have heard that it may be sold for moccasins—cut a steak from its haunches, and leave the huge carcass to smell to heaven for you. It is no better, at least, than to assist at a slaughter house.

The Maine Woods,
"Chesuncook"

I HAVE THE SAME OBJECTION to killing a snake that I have to the killing of any other animal, yet the most humane man that I know never omits to kill one.

Journal
April 26, 1857

IS IT NOT A REPROACH that man is a carnivorous animal? True, he can and does live, in a great measure, by preying on other animals; but this is a miserable way—as any one who will go to snaring rabbits, or slaughtering lambs, may learn—and he will be regarded as a benefactor of his race who shall teach man to confine himself to a more innocent and wholesome diet. Whatever my own practice may be, I have no doubt that it is a part of the destiny of the human race, in its gradual improvement, to leave off eating animals, as surely as the savage tribes have left off eating each other when they came in contact with the more civilized.

Walden, "Higher Laws"

I HAVE FOUND REPEATEDLY, of late years, that I cannot fish without falling a little in self-respect. I have tried it again and again. I have skill at it, and, like many of my fellows, a certain instinct for it, which revives from time to time, but always when I have done I feel that it would have been better if I had not fished. I think that I do not mistake. It is a faint intimation, yet so are the first streaks of morning. There is unquestionably this instinct in me which belongs to the lower orders of creation; yet with every year I am less a fisherman, though without more humanity or even wisdom; at present I am no fisherman at all.

But I see that if I were to live in a wilderness I should again be
tempted to become a fisher and hunter in earnest.

Walden, "Higher Laws"

WHAT A PITIFUL BUSINESS is the fur trade, which has been
pursued now for so many ages, for so many years by famous
companies which enjoy a profitable monopoly and control a
large portion of the earth's surface, unweariedly pursuing and
ferreting out small animals by the aid of all the loafing class
tempted by rum and money, that you may rob some little
fellow-creature of its coat to adorn or thicken your own, that
you may get a fashionable covering in which to hide your head,
or a suitable robe in which to dispense justice to your fellow-
men! Regarded from the philosopher's point of view, it is
precisely on a level with rag and bone picking in the streets of
the cities. The Indian led a more respectable life before he was
tempted to debase himself so much by the white man. Think
how many musquash and weasel skins the Hudson's Bay
Company pile up annually in their warehouses, leaving the
bare red carcasses on the banks of the streams throughout all
British America—and this it is, chiefly, which makes it British
America. It is the place where Great Britain goes a-mousing.
We have heard much of the wonderful intelligence of the
beaver, but that regard for the beaver is all a pretense, and we
would give more for a beaver hat than to preserve the intelligence of the whole race of beavers.

When we see men and boys spend their time shooting and
trapping musquash and mink, we cannot but have a poorer
opinion of them, unless we thought meanly of them before. Yet
the world is imposed on by the fame of the Hudson's Bay and
Northwest Fur Companies, who are only so many partners
more or less in the same sort of business, with thousands of
just such loafing men and boys in their service to abet them.
On the one side is the Hudson's Bay Company, on the other the
company of scavengers who clear the sewers of Paris of their
vermin. There is a good excuse for smoking out or poisoning
rats which infest the house, but when they are as far off as
Hudson's Bay, I think that we had better let them alone. To such

an extent do time and distance, and our imaginations, conse-
crate at last not only the most ordinary, but even vilest
pursuits. The efforts of legislation from time to time to stem
the torrent are significant as showing that there is some sense
and conscience left, but they are insignificant in their effects.
We will fine Abner if he shoots a singing bird, but encourage
the army of Abners that compose the Hudson's Bay Company.

Journal
April 8, 1859

GEORGE MELVIN, OUR CONCORD trapper, told me that in going
to the spring near his house, where he kept his minnows for
bait, he found that they were all gone, and immediately
suspected that a mink had got them; so he removed the snow
all around and laid open the trail of a mink underneath, which
he traced to his hole, where were the fragments of his booty.
There he set his trap, and baited it with fresh minnows. Going
again soon to the spot, he found one of the mink's fore legs in
the trap gnawed off near the body, and, having set it again, he
caught the mink with his three legs, the fourth having only a
short bare bone sticking out.

When I expressed some surprise at this, and said that I
heard of such things but did not know whether to believe them,
and was now glad to have the story confirmed, said he: "Oh, the
muskrats are the greatest fellows to gnaw their legs off. Why, I
caught one once that had just gnawed his third leg off, this
being the third time he had been trapped; and he lay dead by
the trap, for he couldn't run on one leg." Such tragedies are
enacted even in this sphere and along our peaceful streams,
and dignify at least the hunter's trade. Only courage does
anywhere prolong life, whether of man or beast.

When they are caught by the leg and cannot get into the
water to drown themselves, they very frequently gnaw the limb
off. They are commonly caught under water or close to the
edge, and dive immediately with the trap and go to gnawing
and are quackled and drowned in a moment, though under
other circumstances they will live several minutes under water.
They prefer to gnaw off a fore leg to a hind leg, and do not gnaw
off their tails. He says the wharf rats are very common on the

river and will swim and cross it like a muskrat, and will gnaw their legs and even their tails off in the trap.

Journal
1837-1847

No HUMANE BEING, past the thoughtless age of boyhood, will wantonly murder any creature which holds its life by the same tenure that he does.

Walden, "Higher Laws"

THE EXPLORERS AND LUMBERERS generally are all hirelings, paid so much a day for their labor, and as such they have no more love for wild nature than wood-sawyers have for forests. Other white men and Indians who come here are for the most part hunters, whose object is to slay as many moose and other wild animals as possible. But, pray, could not one spend some weeks or years in the solitude of this vast wilderness with other employments than these—employments perfectly sweet and innocent and ennobling? For one that comes with a pencil to sketch or sing, a thousand come with an axe or rifle.

The Maine Woods,
"Chesuncook"

A SERMON IS NEEDED on economy of fuel. What right has my neighbor to burn ten cords of wood, when I burn only one? Thus robbing our half-naked town of this precious covering. Is he so much colder than I? It is expensive to maintain him in our midst. If some earn the salt of their porridge, are we certain that they earn the fuel of their kitchen and parlor? One man makes a little of the driftwood of the river or of the dead and refuse (unmarketable!) wood of the forest suffice, and Nature rejoices in him. Another, Herod-like, requires ten cords of the best of young white oak or hickory, and he is commonly esteemed a virtuous man. He who burns the most wood on his hearth is the least warmed by the sight of it growing. Leave the trim wood-lots to widows and orphan girls. Let men tread gently through nature.

Journal
April 26, 1857

143

NOW IS THE TIME for chestnuts. . . . These gifts should be accepted, not merely with gentleness, but with a certain humble gratitude. The tree whose fruit we would obtain should not be too rudely shaken even. It is not a time of distress, when a little haste and violence even might be pardoned. It is worse than boorish, it is criminal, to inflict an unnecessary injury on the tree that feeds or shadows us. Old trees are our parents, and our parents' parents, perchance. If you would learn the secrets of Nature, you must practice more humanity than others.

Journal
October 23, 1855

I KNOW IT IS A MERE figure of speech to talk about temples nowadays, when men recognize none and associate the word with heathenism. Most men, it appears to me, do not care for Nature, and would sell their share in all her beauty, for as long as they may live, for a stated and not very large sum. Thank God they cannot yet fly and lay waste the sky as well as the earth. We are safe on that side for the present. It is for the very reason that some do not care for these things that we need to combine to protect all from the vandalism of a few.

"Huckleberries"

IF SOME ARE prosecuted for abusing children, others deserve to be prosecuted for maltreating the face of nature committed to their care.

Journal
September 28, 1857

[*Prosecution of land molesters is only an important first step. Our ultimate goal is not to punish, though punish we should, but to prevent. The earth needs our reverence. We need to develop a land-ethic morality to hold dear in our hearts. Our caring for the land—the water downstream, the air downwind, the life all around—must have the force of cherished custom and penalty of public condemnation.*]

SHAD ARE STILL TAKEN in the basin of Concord River, at Lowell, where they are said to be a month earlier than the Merrimack shad, on account of the warmth of the water. Still patiently, almost pathetically, with instinct not to be discouraged, not to be *reasoned* with, revisiting their old haunts, as if their stern fates would relent, and still met by the Corporation with its dam. Poor shad! where is thy redress? When Nature gave thee instinct, gave she thee the heart to bear thy fate? Still wandering the sea in thy scaly armor to inquire humbly at the mouths of rivers if man has perchance left them free for thee to enter. By countless shoals loitering uncertain meanwhile, merely stemming the tide there, in danger from sea foes in spite of thy bright armor, awaiting new instructions, until the sands, until the water itself, tell thee if it be so or not. Thus by whole migrating nations, full of instinct, which is thy faith, in this backward spring, turned adrift, and perchance knowest not where men do *not* dwell, where there are *not* factories, in these days. Armed with no sword, no electric shock, but mere Shad, armed only with innocence and a just cause, with tender dumb mouth only forward, and scales easy to be detached. I for one am with thee, and who knows what may avail a crow-bar against that Billerica dam—Not despairing when whole myriads have gone to feed those sea monsters during thy suspense, but still brave, indifferent, on easy fin there, like shad reserved for higher destinies. . . . Away with the superficial and selfish phil-*anthropy* of men—who knows what admirable virtue of fishes may be below low-water mark, bearing up against a hard destiny, not admired by that fellow-creature who alone can appreciate it! Who hears the fishes when they cry? It will not be forgotten by some memory that we were contemporaries. Thou shalt erelong have thy way up the rivers, up all the rivers of the globe, if I am not mistaken. Yea, even thy dull watery dream shall be more than realized. If it were not so, but thou wert to be overlooked at first and at last, then would not I take their heaven. Yes, I say so, who think I know better than thou canst. Keep a stiff fin then, and stem all the tides thou mayest meet.

A *Week*, "Saturday"

[How apropos. Hayduke Henry: I believe this passage, written in Thoreau's youthful style, is the first advocacy in American history for taking unlawful action to benefit the earth and its nonhuman life. This sort of earth-first endeavor is now known as ecotage or monkey wrenching—a term popularized by Edward Abbey in his novel The Monkey Wrench Gang.]

MEN ATTACH A FALSE importance to celestial phenomena as compared with terrestrial, as if it were more respectable and elevating to watch your neighbors than to mind your own affairs. The nodes of the stars are not the knots we have to untie.

Journal
October 16, 1859

TALK OF HEAVEN! ye disgrace earth.

Walden, "The Ponds"

"A finer utility"

STRANGE THAT SO FEW ever come to the woods to see how the pine lives and grows and spires, lifting its evergreen arms to the light—to see its perfect success; but most are content to behold it in the shape of many broad boards brought to market, and deem *that* its true success! But the pine is no more lumber than man is, and to be made into boards and houses is no more its true and highest use than the truest use of a man is to be cut down and made into manure. There is a higher law affecting our relation to pines as well as to men. A pine cut down, a dead pine, is no more a pine than a dead human carcass is a man. Can he who has discovered only some of the values of whalebone and whale oil be said to have discovered the true use of the whale? Can he who slays the elephant for his ivory be said to have "seen the elephant"? These are petty and accidental uses; just as if a stronger race were to kill us in order to make buttons and flageolets of our bones; for everything may serve a lower as well as a higher use. Every creature is better alive than dead, men and moose and pine-trees, and he who understands it aright will rather preserve its life than destroy it.

Is it the lumberman, then, who is the friend and lover of the pine, stands nearest to it, and understands its nature best? Is it the tanner who has barked it, or he who has boxed it for turpentine, whom posterity will fable to have been changed into a pine at last? No! no! it is the poet; he it is who makes the truest use of the pine—who does not fondle it with an axe, nor tickle it with a saw, nor stroke it with a plane—who knows whether its heart is false without cutting into it—who has not bought the stumpage of the township on which it stands. All the pines shudder and heave a sigh when *that* man steps on the forest floor. No, it is the poet, who loves them as his own shadow in the air, and lets them stand. I have been into the lumber-yard, and the carpenter's shop, and the tannery, and the lampblack factory, and the turpentine clearing; but when at length I saw the tops of the pines waving and reflecting the light at a distance high over all the rest of the forest, I realized that the former were not the highest use of the pine. It is not their bones or hide or tallow that I love most. It is the living spirit of the tree, not its spirit of turpentine, with which I sympathize, and which heals my cuts. It is as immortal as I am, and perchance will go to as high a heaven, there to tower above me still.

> The Maine Woods,
> "Chesuncook"

["It is as immortal as I am, and perchance will go to as high a heaven, there to tower above me still." In 1858 this sentence was as controversial to print as it was courageous to write. In that year James Russell Lowell, afraid such blasphemy would offend orthodox readers, deleted this sentence from Thoreau's article "Chesuncook." Outraged, Thoreau wrote Lowell, then editor of the Atlantic Monthly, demanding that the omitted sentence be published in a succeeding issue. Henry waited for four months—Lowell ignored his wish. Thoreau then requested payment and refused future contribution to the Atlantic Monthly. Thoreau's pine-tree sentence, an early progenitor of today's "trees have standing" phrase, was not printed until The Maine Woods was published in 1864, two years after his death.]

BEAUTY IS A FINER utility whose end we do not see.

Journal
September 29, 1842

THIS CURIOUS WORLD which we inhabit is more wonderful than it is convenient; more beautiful than it is useful; it is more to be admired and enjoyed than used.

Commencement Address
August 16, 1837

A FARMER ONCE ASKED me what shrub oaks were made for, not knowing any use they served. But I can tell him that they do me good. They are my parish ministers, regularly settled. They never did any man harm that I know.

Journal
December 17, 1856

[Unfortunately, mankind still asks that awful question—"What's it good for"—of a nonhuman life. That very question, insidious as it is, however, represents an improvement in consciousness. For historical perspective we should remember the words of Puritan Cotton Mather, possessor of the *largest library in seventeenth-century colonial America, who preached and wrote, "What is not useful is vicious."*

The fact that many people now find that question openly repugnant, and reject the anthropocentrism it implies, is a great stride forward in our evolving relationship with nonhuman life. These people realize the spinning earth is not our lazy susan. They believe life—whales, wolverines, prairie chickens, pine trees, toads, nematodes—has inherent worth, is good in and of itself, needs no economic justification of value, no human rationale for its continued existence.]

IF A MAN WALK in the woods for love of them half of each day, he is in danger of being regarded as a loafer; but if he spends his whole day as a speculator, shearing off those woods and making earth bald before her time, he is esteemed an industrious and enterprising citizen. As if a town had no interest in its forests but to cut them down!

"Life without Principle"

DOES HE CHIEFLY own the land who coldly uses it and gets corn and potatoes out of it, or he who loves it and gets inspiration from it?

Journal
April 23, 1857

PRATT, WHEN I TOLD HIM of this nest, said he would like to carry one of his rifles down there. But I told him that I should be sorry to have them killed. I would rather save one of these hawks than have a hundred hens and chickens. It was worth more to see them soar, especially now that they are so rare in the landscape. It is easy to buy eggs, but not to buy hen-hawks. My neighbors would not hesitate to shoot the last pair of hen-hawks in the town to save a few of their chickens! But such economy is narrow and grovelling. It is unnecessary to sacrifice the greater value to the less. I would rather never taste chickens' meat nor hens' eggs than never to see a hawk sailing through the upper air again. This sight is worth incomparably more than a chicken soup or a boiled egg. So we exterminate the deer and substitute the hog. It was amusing to observe the swaying to and fro of the young hawk's head to counterbalance the gentle motion of the bough in the wind.

Journal
June 13, 1853

[This is the earliest sentiment supporting protection of birds of prey— predators of any type in fact—that I have found. Many prominent naturalists, in the late 1800s and well into the 1900s, still urged birdwatchers and others to take sides, to shoot hawks to protect songbirds.

Prior to 1934, when the Hawk Mountain Sanctuary (Pennsylvania) was established, gunners slaughtered thousands upon thousands of hawks, eagles and falcons as they funneled low along the Hawk Mountain ridgeline during fall migration. Federal legislation granted protection to all birds of prey in 1972.]

WHEN THE QUESTION of the protection of birds comes up, the legislatures regard only a low use and never a high use; the best-disposed legislators employ one, perchance, only to examine their crops and see how many grubs or cherries they contain, and never to study their dispositions, or the beauty of their plumage, or listen and report on the sweetness of their song. The legislature will preserve a bird professedly not because it is a beautiful creature, but because it is a good scavenger or the like. This, at least, is the defense set up. It is as if the question were whether some celebrated singer of the human race—some Jenny Lind or another—did more harm or good, should be destroyed, or not, and therefore a committee should be appointed, not to listen to her singing at all, but to examine the contents of her stomach and see if she devoured anything which was injurious to the farmers and gardeners, or which they cannot spare.

Journal
April 18, 1859

IN MY BOATING OF LATE I have several times scared up a couple of summer ducks of this year, bred in our meadows. They allowed me to come quite near, and helped to people the river. I have not seen them for some days. Would you know the end of our intercourse? Goodwin shot them, and Mrs. ——, who never sailed on the river, ate them. Of course, she knows not what she did. What if I should eat her canary? Thus we share each other's sins as well as burdens. The lady who watches admiringly the matador shares his deed. They belonged to me, as much as to anyone, when they were alive, but it was considered of more importance that Mrs. —— should taste the flavor of them dead than that I should enjoy the beauty of them alive.

Journal
August 16, 1858

WE BOAST OF OUR system of education, but why stop at schoolmasters and schoolhouses? We are all schoolmasters and our schoolhouse is the universe. To attend chiefly to the desk or schoolhouse, while we neglect the scenery in which it is placed, is absurd. If we do not look out we shall find our fine schoolhouse standing in a cow yard at last.

"Huckleberries"

IF ANYBODY ELSE—any farmer, at least—should spend an hour thus wading about here in this secluded swamp, barelegged, intent on the sphagnum, filling his pocket only, with no rake in his hand and no bag or bushel on the bank, he would be pronounced insane and have a guardian put over him; but if he'll spend his time skimming and watering his milk and selling his small potatoes for large ones, or generally in skinning flints, he will probably be made guardian of some-body else. I have not garnered any rye or oats, but I gathered the wild vine of the Assabet.

Journal
August 30, 1856

YET WHAT IS THE CHARACTER of our gratitude to these squirrels, these planters of forests? We regard them as vermin, and annually shoot and destroy them in great numbers, because—if we have any excuse—they sometimes devour a little of our Indian corn, while, perhaps, they are planting the nobler oak-corn (acorn) in its place. In various parts of the country an army of grown-up boys assembles for a squirrel hunt. They choose sides, and the side that kills the greatest number of thousands enjoys a supper at the expense of the other side, and the whole neighborhood rejoices. Would it not be far more civilized and humane, not to say godlike, to recognize once in the year by some significant symbolical ceremony the part which the squirrel plays, the great service it performs, in the economy of the universe?

Journal
October 22, 1860

IT IS REMARKABLE THAT many men will go with eagerness to Walden Pond in the winter to fish for pickerel and yet not seem to care for the landscape. Of course it cannot be *merely* for the pickerel they may catch: there is some adventure in it; but any love of nature which they may feel is certainly very slight and indefinite. They call it going a-fishing, and so indeed it is, though, perchance, their natures know better. Now I go a-fishing and a-hunting every day, but omit the fish and the game, which are the least important part. I have learned to do without them. They were indispensable only as long as I was a boy. I am encouraged when I see a dozen villagers drawn to Walden Pond to spend a day in fishing through the ice, and suspect that I have more fellows than I knew, but I am disappointed and surprised to find that they lay all the stress on the fish which they catch or fail to catch, and on nothing else, as if there were nothing else to be caught.

Journal
January 26, 1853

WE CUT DOWN THE FEW old oaks which witnessed the transfer of the township from the Indian to the white man, and perchance commence our museum with a cartridge box taken from a British soldier in 1775. How little we insist on truly grand and beautiful natural features. There may be the most beautiful landscapes in the world within a dozen miles of us, for aught we know—for their inhabitants do not value nor perceive them—and so have not made them known to others—but if a grain of gold were picked up there, or a pearl found in a freshwater clam, the whole state would resound with the news.

"Huckleberries"

You would say that some men had been tempted to live in this world at all only by the offer of a bounty by the general government—a bounty on living—to any one who will consent to be *out* at this era of the world, the object of the governors being to create a nursery for their navy. I told such a man the other day that I had got a Canada lynx here in Concord, and his instant question was, "Have you got the reward for him?" What reward? Why, the ten dollars which the State offers. As long as I saw him he neither said nor thought anything about the lynx, but only about this reward. "Yes," said he, "this State offers ten dollars reward." You might have inferred that ten dollars was something rarer in his neighborhood than a lynx even, and he was anxious to see it on that account. I have thought that a lynx was a bright-eyed, four-legged, furry beast of the cat kind, very *current*, indeed, though its natural gait is by leaps. But he knew it to be a draught drawn by the cashier of the wildcat bank on the State treasury, payable at sight. Then I reflected that the first money was of leather, or a whole creature (whence *pecunia*, from *pecus*, a herd), and, since leather was at first furry, I easily understood the connection between a lynx and ten dollars, and found that all money was traceable right back to the original wildcat bank. But the fact was that, instead of receiving ten dollars for the lynx which I had got, I had paid away some dollars in order to get him. So, you see, I was away back in a gray antiquity behind the institution of money—further than history goes.

This reminded me that I once saw a cougar recently killed at the Adirondacks which had had its ears clipped. This was a ten-dollar cougar.

Journal
November 29, 1860

White Pond and Walden are great crystals on the surface of the earth, Lakes of Light. If they were permanently congealed, and small enough to be clutched, they would, perchance, be carried off by slaves, like precious stones, to adorn the heads of emperors; but being liquid, and ample, and secured to us and our successors forever, we disregard them, and run after the diamond of Kohinoor. They are too pure to have a market value; they contain no muck. How much more beautiful than our lives, how much more transparent than our characters, are they! We never learned meanness of them. How much fairer than the pool before the farmer's door, in which his ducks swim! Hither the clean wild ducks come.

Walden, "The Ponds"

"Let us improve our opportunities"

I STAND IN EBBY HUBBARD'S yellow birch swamp, admiring some gnarled and shaggy picturesque old birches there, which send out large knee-like limbs near the ground, while the brook, raised by the late rain, winds fuller than usual through the rocky swamp. I thought with regret how soon these trees, like the black birches that grew on the hill near by, would be all cut off, and there would be almost nothing of the old Concord left, and we should be reduced to read old deeds in order to be reminded of such things—deeds, at least, in which some old and revered bound trees are mentioned. These will be the only proof at last that they ever existed. Pray, farmers, keep some old woods to match the old deeds. Keep them for history's sake, as specimens of what the township was. Let us not be reduced to a mere paper evidence, to deeds kept in a chest or secretary, when not so much as the bark of the paper birch will be left for evidence, about its decayed stump.

Journal
November 8, 1858

AT PRESENT, IN THIS VICINITY, the best part of the land is not private property; the landscape is not owned, and the walker enjoys comparative freedom. But possibly the day will come when it will be partitioned off into so-called pleasure-grounds, in which a few will take a narrow and exclusive pleasure only—when fences shall be multiplied, and man-traps and other engines invented to confine men to the *public* road, and walking over the surface of God's earth shall be construed to mean trespassing on some gentleman's grounds. To enjoy a thing exclusively is commonly to exclude yourself from the true enjoyment of it. Let us improve our opportunities, then, before the evil days come.

"Walking"

I THINK THAT EACH TOWN should have a park, or rather a primitive forest, of five hundred or a thousand acres, either in one body or several—where a stick should never be cut for fuel—nor for the navy, nor to make wagons, but stand and decay for higher uses—a common possession forever, for instruction and recreation.

All Walden wood might have been reserved, with Walden in the midst of it, and the Easterbrooks country, an uncultivated area of some four square miles in the north of the town, might have been our huckleberry field. If any owners of these tracts are about to leave the world without natural heirs who need or deserve to be specially remembered, they will do wisely to abandon the possession to all mankind, and not will them to some individual who perhaps has enough already—and so correct the error that was made when the town was laid out. As some give to Harvard College or another Institution, so one might give a forest or a huckleberry field to Concord. This town surely is an institution which deserves to be remembered.

"Huckleberries"

[*Thoreau's specific conservation wishes for the Concord area have, in small measure, come true. Walden wood was preserved in 1922, when the 355-acre Walden Pond State Reservation was established. (A trail leads to the*

site of his hut, gone but marked simply, as Henry would have liked it, with
an ever-growing pile of rocks placed in tribute.) Harvard University
acquired 670 acres of the Easterbrook country—Easterbrook Nature
Preserve—in 1967.]

AMONG THE INDIANS, the earth and its productions generally
were common and free to all the tribe, like the air and water—
but among us who have supplanted the Indians, the public
retain only a small yard or common in the middle of the village,
with perhaps a grave-yard beside it, and the right of way, by
sufferance, by a particular narrow route, which is annually
becoming narrower, from one such yard to another. . . . This is
the way we civilized men have arranged it.

I am not overflowing with respect and gratitude to the
fathers who thus laid out our New England villages, whatever
precedent they were influenced by, for I think that a 'prentice
hand liberated from Old English prejudices could have done
much better in this new world. If they were in earnest seeking
thus far away 'freedom to worship God,' as some assure us—
why did they not secure a little more of it, when it was so cheap
and they were about it? At the same time that they built
meeting-houses why did they not preserve from desecration
and destruction far grander temples not made with hands?

"Huckleberries"

NATURE HAS A PLACE for the wild clematis as well as for the
cabbage.

"Walking"

IT IS TRUE WE AS YET take liberties and go across lots, and steal,
or "hook," a good many things, but we naturally take fewer and
fewer liberties every year, as we meet with more resistance. In
old countries, as England, going across lots is out of the
question. You must walk in some beaten path or other, though
it may be a narrow one. We are tending to the same state of
things here, when practically a few will have grounds of their
own, but most will have none to walk over but what the few
allow them.

Thus we behave like oxen in a flower-garden. The true fruit of Nature can only be plucked with a delicate hand not bribed by any earthly reward, and a fluttering heart. No hired man can help us to gather this crop.

Journal
January 3, 1861

METHINKS THE TOWN should have more supervision and control over its parks than it has. It concerns us all whether these proprietors choose to cut down all the woods this winter or not.

Journal
January 22, 1852

[I have no proof that this viewpoint was the first of its kind in our country, but I am convinced it was among the earliest recommendations to control unlimited cutting (bulldozing now) in an essentially urban environment. In this regard, unfortunately, Henry is still far ahead of his time.

Despite the advocacy by urban foresters, and despite growing environmental problems of global proportions, most cities in our country have yet to enact "tree ordinances," as they are generically called. These green laws would require developers, and others, to spare a specified number of trees per lot or acre. Ideally, trees should be protected for their own sake, and the sake of the life—birds, mammals, insects, etc.—they support. But since city councils are anthropocentric by definition, trees could also be preserved to enhance the beauty (pleasure, money) of our communities, to filter noise and air pollution (health) and to moderate summer heat (comfort, money), especially in our big cities where the "heat island" effect is becoming so unbearable. And they could also be saved so that they could continue their CPR work: oxygen, life.]

A VILLAGE NEEDS THESE innocent stimulants of bright and cheering prospects to keep off melancholy and superstition. Show me two villages, one embowered in trees and blazing with all the glories of October, the other a merely trivial and treeless waste, or with only a single tree or two for suicides, and I shall be sure that in the latter will be found the most starved and bigoted religionists and the most desperate drinkers. Every wash-tub and milk-can and gravestone will be exposed.

The inhabitants will disappear abruptly behind their barns and houses, like desert Arabs amid their rocks, and I shall look to see spears in their hands. They will be ready to accept the most barren and forlorn doctrine—as that the world is speedily coming to an end, or has already got to it, or that they themselves are turned wrong side outward. They will perchance crack their dry joints at one another and call it a spiritual communication.

But to confine ourselves to the Maples. What if we were to take half as much pains in protecting them as we do in setting them out—not stupidly tie our horses to our dahlia stems?

"Autumnal Tints"

I THINK OF NO NATURAL FEATURE which is a greater ornament and treasure to this town than the river. It is one of the things which determine whether a man will live here or in another place, and it is one of the first objects which we show to a stranger. In this respect we enjoy a great advantage over those neighboring towns which have no river. Yet the town, as a corporation, has never turned any but the most purely utilitarian eyes upon it—and has done nothing to preserve its natural beauty.

They who laid out the town should have made the river available as a common possession forever. The town collectively should at least have done as much as an individual of taste who owns an equal area commonly does in England. Indeed I think that not only the channel but one or both banks of every river should be a public highway—for a river is not useful merely to float on. In this case, one bank might have been reserved as a public walk and the trees that adorned it have been protected, and frequent avenues have been provided leading to it from the main street. This would have cost but a few acres of land and but little wood, and we should all have been gainers by it. Now it is accessible only at the bridges at points comparatively distant from the town, and there there is not a foot of shore to stand on unless you trespass on somebody's lot—and if you attempt a quiet stroll down the bank—you soon meet with fences built at right angles with the stream and projecting far over the water—where individuals, naturally enough, under the present arrangement—seek to monopolize the shore. At last we shall get our only view of the stream from the meeting house belfry.

As for the trees which fringed the shore within my remembrance—where are they? and where will the remnant of them be after ten years more?

"Huckleberries"

[*Again, I have no proof that this proposal was the first of its kind in our country, but am certain it was among the earliest recommendations to preserve the natural beauty of rivers and streams—to establish greenways—in or near our urban areas. Across the country, commissions are discovering ways and means to provide riverside recreation and protect floodplain forests, which provide habitat and dispersal corridors for wildlife. I am proud to say that my home county of Clarke (Georgia) completed its first greenway trail in 1990.*

The fact that our attitudes toward urban waterways are finally changing demonstrates the value of proposing preservation early, often and persistently. This plus the leadership of a few earnest men and women forces change.]

WHAT ARE THE NATURAL features which make a township handsome? A river, with its waterfalls and meadows, a lake, a hill, a cliff or individual rocks, a forest, and ancient trees standing singly. Such things are beautiful; they have a high use which dollars and cents never represent. If the inhabitants of a town were wise, they would seek to preserve these things, though at a considerable expense; for such things educate far more than any hired teachers or preachers, or any at present recognized system of school education. I do not think him fit to be the founder of a state or even of a town who does not foresee the use of these things, but legislates chiefly for oxen, as it were.

Journal
January 3, 1861

IF THE PEOPLE OF MASSACHUSETTS are ready to found a professorship of Natural History—so they must see the importance of preserving some portions of nature herself unimpaired.

I find that the rising generation in this town do not know what an oak or a pine is, having seen only inferior specimens. Shall we hire a man to lecture on botany, on oaks for instance, our noblest plants—while we permit others to cut down the few best specimens of these trees that are left? It is like teaching children Latin and Greek while we burn the books printed in those languages.

"Huckleberries"

THE KINGS OF ENGLAND formerly had their forests "to hold the king's game," for sport or food, sometimes destroying villages to create or extend them; and I think that they were impelled by a true instinct. Why should not we, who have renounced the king's authority, have our national preserves, where no villages need be destroyed, in which the bear and panther, and some even of the hunter race, may still exist, and not be "civilized off the face of the earth"—our forests, not to hold the king's game merely, . . . not for idle sport or food, but for inspiration and our own true recreation? or shall we, like the villains, grub them all up, poaching on our own national domains?

The Maine Woods,
"Chesuncook"

[Thoreau made his second expedition to the Maine wilderness in 1853. By that time all of the incredible stands of white pine near the streams and lakes had already been cut. Every large lake he paddled across was dammed to float logs. Many of the men he met had come to the woods to kill moose for money. "Chesuncook" was his reaction.

Written primarily in 1853 and 1854, the near book-length article "Chesuncook" was not published until it appeared in the Atlantic Monthly in 1858. At the time many thought Thoreau's "national preserve" proposal was the first of its kind. Today, however, George Catlin, the renowned painter of western Indians, is usually credited as the first to dream of the national park concept. Thoreau's recommendation, independent of Catlin's and more widely read, was second.

The Congress of the United States passed legislation, signed by President Grant, authorizing the world's first national park—Yellowstone—in 1872.]

THOUSANDS ANNUALLY SEEK the White Mountains to be refreshed by their wild and primitive beauty—but when the
country was discovered a similar kind of beauty prevailed all
over it—and much of this might have been preserved for our
present refreshment if a little foresight and taste had been
used.

I do not believe that there is a town in this country which
realizes in what its true wealth consists.

I visited the town of Boxboro only eight miles west of us
last fall—and far the handsomest and most memorable thing
which I saw there, was its noble oak wood. I doubt if there is a
finer one in Massachusetts. Let it stand fifty years longer and
men will make pilgrimages to it from all parts of the country,
and for a worthier object than to shoot squirrels in it—and yet
I said to myself, Boxboro would be very like the rest of New
England, if she were ashamed of that wood-land. Probably, if
the history of this town is written, the historian will have
omitted to say a word about this forest—the most interesting
thing in it—and lay all the stress on the history of the parish.

"Huckleberries"

IT WOULD BE WORTH THE WHILE if in each town there were a
committee appointed to see that the beauty of the town
received no detriment. If we have the largest boulder in the
county, then it should not belong to an individual, nor be made
into door-steps.

As in many countries precious metals belong to the crown,
so here more precious natural objects of rare beauty should
belong to the public.

Not only the channel but one or both banks of every river
should be a public highway. The only use of a river is not to float
on it.

Think of a mountain-top in the township—even to the
minds of the Indians a sacred place—only accessible through
private grounds! a temple, as it were, which you cannot enter
except by trespassing and at the risk of letting out or letting in
somebody's cattle! in fact the temple itself in this case private
property and standing in a man's cow-yard—for such is com-

monly the case!

New Hampshire courts have lately been deciding—as if it was for them to decide—whether the top of Mt. Washington belonged to A or to B; and, it being decided in favor of B, as I hear, he went up one winter with the proper officer and took formal possession of it. But I think that the top of Mt. Washington should not be private property; it should be left unappropriated for modesty and reverence's sake, or if only to suggest that earth has higher uses than we put her to.

Journal
January 3, 1861

[*Mount Washington, New England's highest peak (6,288 ft.), is no longer a private possession. The mountain, including the remainder of the Presidential Range, has transcended to its highest use as part of the public domain—the White Mountain National Forest, established in 1912. For more than 50 years the Appalachian Trail has rollercoastered across the rocky crest of the Presidentials, free for the effort.*]

NATURE IS STRONGER than law, and the sure but slow influence of wind and water will balk the efforts of restricting legislatures. Man cannot set up bounds with safety but where the revolutions of nature will confirm and strengthen, not obliterate, them.

Journal
October 1842

WE ARE A YOUNG PEOPLE and have not learned by experience the consequence of cutting off the forest. One day they will be planted, methinks, and nature reinstated to some extent.

Journal
September 4, 1851

MAN'S WORKS MUST LIE in the bosom of Nature, cottages be buried in trees, or under vines and moss, like rocks, that they may not outrage the landscape. The hunter must be dressed in Lincoln green, with a plume of eagle's feathers, to imbosom him in Nature. So the skillful painter secures the distinctness of the whole by the indistinctness of the parts. We can endure best to consider our repose and silence. Only when the city, the hamlet, or the cottage is viewed from a distance does man's life seem in harmony with the universe; but seen closely his actions have no eagle's feathers or Lincoln green to redeem them. The sunlight on cities at a distance is a deceptive beauty, but foretells the final harmony of man with Nature.

Journal
March 7-10, 1841

Moose . . .

. . . Indians

Bibliography

Blake, H. G. O., ed. *The Writings of Henry David Thoreau*. Riverside Edition. Vols. 1-9. Boston: Houghton Mifflin, 1893.

Duncan, Jeffrey L. *Thoreau: The Major Essays*. New York: Dutton, 1972.

Thoreau, Henry David. *Henry David Thoreau: The Natural History Essays*. Salt Lake City: Peregrine Smith, 1980.

_____ . *The Writings of Henry David Thoreau*. Concord Edition. Vols. 1-6. Boston: Houghton Mifflin, 1906. Vol. 5, *Excursions and Poems*, includes "A Yankee in Canada."

Torrey, Bradford, and Francis H. Allen, eds. *The Journal of Henry David Thoreau*. 14 vols. Walden edition. Forward by Henry Seidel Canby. Boston: Houghton Mifflin, 1949.

Recommended Reading

Bode, Carl, ed. *The Portable Thoreau*. New York: Viking, 1964.

Houde, Carl F., et al., eds. *The Illustrated "A Week on the Concord and Merrimack Rivers."* Photographs from the Gleason Collection. Princeton: Princeton Univ. Press, 1983.

Howarth, William, commentator. *Thoreau in the Mountains: Writings by Henry David Thoreau*. New York: Farrar, Straus, Giroux, 1982.

Krutch, Joseph W., ed. *Walden and Other Writings by Henry David Thoreau*. Toronto: Bantam, 1981.

Moldenhauer, Joseph J., ed. *The Illustrated "Maine Woods."* Photographs from the Gleason Collection. Princeton: Princeton Univ. Press, 1974.

Porter, Eliot, ed. & photographer. *In Wildness*. San Francisco: Sierra Club, 1962.

Shepard, Odell, ed. *The Heart of Thoreau's Journals*. Boston: Houghton Mifflin, 1923.

Thoreau, Henry David. *Cape Cod: Henry David Thoreau's Complete Text, with the Journey Recreated in Pictures by William F. Robinson*. Boston: Little, Brown, 1985.